THE KEYS
to Planning
for Learning

Effective Curriculum, Unit, and Lesson Design

DONNA CLEMENTI AND LAURA TERRILL

The American Council on the Teaching of Foreign Languages
1001 North Fairfax Street, Suite 200
Alexandria, VA 22314

Graphic Design by Goulah Design Group, Inc.
Edited by Sandy Cutshall, Print Management, Inc.

© 2013 by The American Council on the Teaching of Foreign Languages, Alexandria, VA

Graphic for Curriculum Design for Learning Languages in the 21st Century (Figures 1, 6, and 14)
used with permission of designers, Donna Clementi and Laura Terrill.

LinguaFolio® is a registered trademark of the National Council of State Supervisors
for Languages (NCSSFL).

ISBN: 978-0-9896532-2-0

Foreword

Our learners need "right now" schools with "right now" teachers. The 21st century is well into its second decade and educators are searching for guidance on how to construct dynamic curriculum and instruction to match our times. Given the remarkable pedagogical shifts occurring with access to digital tools, media production, and instantaneous connectivity, teachers seek "keys" to open the future for our students. World language learning, which supports global sensibilities and superb communication skills, provides a foundation for the contemporary learner. To assist teachers, curriculum designers, administrators, and professional developers, Donna Clementi and Laura Terrill have indeed brought us a useful guide—*The Keys to Planning for Learning: Effective Curriculum, Unit, and Lesson Design.*

Bringing years of experience in language teaching, district and organizational leadership, and teacher development to these chapters, Clementi and Terrill provide powerful strategies for rebooting teaching and learning. In many ways, curriculum design is a form of learning architecture. I believe it is here that our authors help teachers in the most direct and intimate way. Like architects, teachers make critical choices about the elements, the layout, the construction, the materials, and the style that will best serve the client and meet local standards. For today's language teacher, strategies to assist in these choices are valued. The chapters are written in a logical sequence and provide clarity as to why and how to integrate the five goal areas of the National Standards for Learning Languages (Communication, Cultures, Connections, Comparisons, and Communities) into classroom planning. In particular, the unit design and supportive lesson plan templates are excellent blueprints for dealing with two simultaneous needs for designers. One is to support excellent interpersonal, interpretive, and presentational communication (listening, speaking, reading, and writing) in a world language and the second need is to engage our students in expanding their knowledge and appreciation of cultural perspectives.

As a futurist, I encourage the reader to note that this book is written for the "now." Clementi and Terrill not only are keenly aware of the necessary skills and knowledge that our times require of our learners, they embrace them with fresh writing on the "mindset" for curriculum writing in our times. *The Keys to Planning for Learning: Effective Curriculum, Unit, and Lesson Design* will prove to be an outstanding contribution as a launching pad into the future of world language teaching and learning.

Heidi Hayes Jacobs
President, Curriculum Designers, Inc.
Author of *Interdisciplinary Curriculum: Design and Implementation* and
Curriculum 21: Essential Education for A Changing World

Introduction

Learning a language is far more than an intellectual, cognitive challenge.
It is a means to grow and mature through the experience of other
cultures. It gives breadth and depth to our personalities. It allows us to
approach problems differently because we have experienced different
worlds; it allows us, as Proust says, to see with new eyes.

— Veroncia Lacey

As we wrote *The Keys to Planning for Learning: Effective Curriculum, Unit, and Lesson Design* we strived to capture what is known about best practices from general educational research as well as what is known from research that is specific to language learning. This book is not intended to convey how teachers might do things better, but rather is intended to focus the discussion on how we might do things differently given the need to support learners as they acquire the skills needed for a future that cannot be easily imagined. We have taken the liberty to suggest best practices and strategies based on our combined 50+ years of experience in classrooms K–12, our work with pre-service teachers in methods courses, and countless hours engaged in conversations and workshops with other dedicated professionals about what works and what doesn't work in the classroom. The process for curriculum, unit, and lesson design shared here reflects the following beliefs:

- The learner is at the center of all that we do. The world language curriculum is dynamic and must be dynamic to accommodate the increased diversity of learners and the ways that they are learning and are able to learn languages.

- The Standards for Learning Languages provide broad content goals that can be tailored to the developmental needs and special interests of the learner, and to specific program model requirements. The ACTFL Proficiency Guidelines provide the pathway of progress to greater facility in communication skills.

- A dynamic world language curriculum forges connections between and among the other disciplines allowing learners to explore interesting questions and issues while acquiring linguistic and cultural proficiency. The ideas that surface as learners explore interesting topics spark the imagination and creativity of the learner, allowing learners to explore creative solutions to identified problems.

- Language is retained when it is acquired in a meaningful context; one that allows learners to use their developing language skills to learn about, interact with, and influence their world at home, in their communities, and globally.

The mindset for curriculum, unit, and lesson design presented here offers one way to structure and organize curriculum, instruction, and assessment. We know that there are other effective models. It is our hope that the ideas expressed in this book will spark conversation and continued dialogue about how to best meet the needs of today's language learners at all levels of instruction. It is our intent to make the website for this publication a place where we can collaborate with others to showcase units for all languages at all levels.

—Donna Clementi and Laura Terrill

The Keys to Planning for Learning

Acknowledgments

The desire to connect with and learn from others has been part of both of our careers since we started in the profession. In that spirit, we would like to acknowledge those groups and organizations that have greatly influenced our thinking. Special recognition goes to our colleagues in our local school districts and state organizations in Missouri and Wisconsin. They ensured that we were challenged from early in our careers to make language learning purposeful and meaningful. Our involvement with other organizations—ACTFL, CARLA, Concordia Language Villages, CSCTFL, NNELL, NADSFL—allowed us to continue to grow professionally.

We would like to recognize Marie Trayer who served as Project Coordinator for the development of the 1996 Nebraska K–12 Foreign Language Frameworks. This body of work and the workshops presented by Dr. Trayer were pivotal in shaping how we approached curriculum development as teachers and leaders in subsequent years.

Appreciation and thanks to all of our teaching colleagues, our student teachers in our methods courses, and to our many workshop participants. You challenged us with your thoughtful questions; many ideas that are now part of this book resulted from those rich discussions.

We are indebted to those who helped to bring this book to completion:

- Our excellent reviewers—Leslie Baldwin, Adriana Brandt, Michael Everson and Cherice Montgomery. Your comments were extremely helpful and informed the final version of this book.

- ACTFL leadership—Executive Director Marty Abbott and Director of Education Paul Sandrock. Your insights and suggestions throughout the writing process greatly influenced the contents of this *Keys* publication.

Finally, a very special thanks to our families who were willing to let us do what we needed and wanted to do both when writing this book and throughout our careers. It would not have been possible to do this without their love and support.

—Donna Clementi and Laura Terrill

Table of Contents

Resources for *The Keys to Planning for Learning* are available at the ACTFL website (www.actfl.org/publications/books-and-brochures/the-keys-planning-learning), including:

- All material in the Appendixes
- Blank templates to download for curriculum, unit, and lesson design
- Access to materials or documents referenced in the publication
- Sample units for different languages and levels

Chapter 1 | 21st Century World Languages Curriculum

Education is the kindling of a flame, not the filling of a vessel.

— Socrates

Who Are Today's Learners and What Do They Need?

Diversity is the first word that comes to mind when thinking of today's learners. While they share many characteristics, they are still uniquely individual with diverse needs. They come from a variety of backgrounds and bring different languages and cultures to our classrooms. They come from lives of privilege and poverty. They live in rural, urban, and suburban communities. Some have never left their community and others have traveled the world either virtually or literally. Some have strong support at home and others are facing the world on their own. Our first priority as world language educators must be to create a strong sense of community in our classrooms so that learners feel comfortable in their first attempts to communicate in another language, encouraged to ask questions when they don't understand, supported in their exploration of new perspectives. Then, we can focus on the knowledge and skills that these learners need in order to participate successfully in the 21st century.

Let's begin with the profile of the 21st century learner. In 2012, Google/Ipsos Media CT published the results of a study about the media habits of youth between the ages of 13 and 24 (www.google.com/think/research-studies/media-habits-of-teens-and-twenty-somethings-2012.html). They identified the following characteristics about this group:

- Almost 8 in 10 take action after seeing an online ad, including searching for more information or visiting a website.
- 35% use their PC, smartphone, and TV at the same time.
- 92% engage with at least two devices simultaneously—including TVs, PCs, smartphones, and tablets.
- 71% search for information online after seeing a topic of interest on television.
- 76% use devices sequentially, looking for information on a smartphone and then using a PC to find more information.
- 45% use a smartphone to access online resources and content.
- 8.2 hours a week are spent online on smartphones.

What do these data suggest? First, they make it clear that schools are just one of the places where students can learn. Learners are using technologies that allow them to learn what they want, when they want, and where they want. In terms of language learning, today's learners can point a scanner at a sign and hear the message read to them at any speed in a variety of languages. While reading an article online, they can click and receive a translation in several languages. They can sign up for free daily language lessons. They can connect with someone halfway around the world to practice the language they are learning.

The data also suggest that learners are naturally curious. When something captures their interest, they will investigate the topic further using the resources that are immediately available. Finally, the data suggest that learners are multi-taskers who believe that they can attend to more than one thing at a time. As learners, they are likely to become impatient when put in situations where they are required to focus on a single prescribed topic, and frustrated when they are not able to be hyper-connected. They do not like to wait for results. These digital natives are more engaged in classes where teachers:

- design authentic tasks built around discovery and problem solving;
- build in time and space for them (the learners) to explore their own interests and questions within a unit of study;
- facilitate inquiry, exploration, and collaboration among learners;
- allow choice in how to demonstrate they have met the unit goals and objectives; and
- provide ongoing feedback as they work independently and in small groups.

Successful participation in our 21st century global community requires that language learners possess sophisticated skills and knowledge. The opportunities to actively use the target language and related cultural understandings beyond the classroom and throughout life have increased significantly due to global links via technology that occur daily in our lives. No longer does physical location on the world map dictate the potential for communication with someone from another country and/or someone who speaks a language other than English. Learners need to develop real-world skills they can use throughout their work, career, and personal lives.

How Does a 21st Century Curriculum Address the Needs of Today's Learners?

For learners to develop real-world communication skills, curriculum cannot be designed in isolation. It must be designed in tandem with instructional strategies, and assessment of and for learning to ensure that the learners can communicate using the target language purposefully in real-life situations. *Standards for Foreign Language Learning in the 21st Century 3rd Edition Revised* (NSFLEP, 2006) (see Appendix A) includes this statement: "To study another language and culture gives one the powerful key to successful communication: *knowing how, when, and why, to say what to whom.* All the linguistic and social knowledge required for effective human-to-human interaction is encompassed in those ten words" (p. 11). This is the overarching, enduring understanding related to the discipline of world language study.

Given the reality that young people in the United States who do study a language other than English do not all begin at the same age, continue for the same amount of time, or learn the language via the same program model, a guide for world language cannot dictate specific content choices. What can be prescribed is a foundation upon which curricula for learning world languages can be designed. This foundation includes two components: the Standards for Learning Languages (2006), and the American Council on the Teaching of Foreign Languages (ACTFL) Proficiency Guidelines (2012a) (see Appendix B). Figure 1 represents an image of curriculum design for learning languages in the 21st century.

Figure 1. Curriculum Design for Learning Languages in the 21st Century

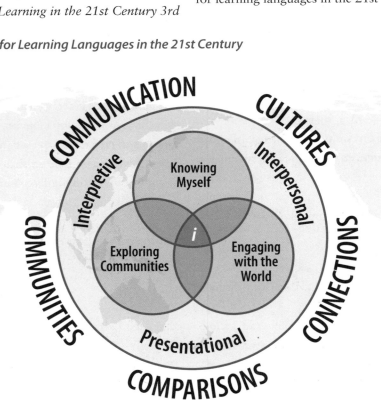

All world languages curricula, regardless of program model, are based on the goal of working towards proficiency in the three modes of communication: interpersonal, interpretive, and presentational. The pathway to proficiency moves learners from understanding and producing words, phrases, and short memorized sentences to creating personal meaning with and through the language and, ultimately, to understanding and producing paragraph-length narration on a wide variety of topics. The Venn diagram within the communication circle reminds us that a unit theme or topic should relate to the learner on a personal level (*Knowing Myself*), to where the learner lives locally, regionally, nationally (*Exploring Communities*), and globally (*Engaging with the World*). Surrounding the image are the 5 Cs of the Standards for Learning Languages—Communication, Cultures, Connections, Comparisons, Communities—that guide choices of content. In the center of the Venn diagram is an *"i"* representing *Interculturality*:

> *Interculturality* is the interaction of people from different cultural backgrounds using authentic language appropriately in a way that demonstrates knowledge and understanding of the cultures. It is the ability to experience the culture of another person and to be open-minded, interested, and curious about that person and culture. Language learners must be able to evaluate personal feelings, thoughts, perceptions, and reactions in order to understand another culture and use that experience to reflect on their own life and surroundings. (www.learnNC.org)

The image of world language curriculum (Figure 1) is intended to show how language and culture are inextricably linked, and how the learner's interactions with people who speak other languages and/or come from diverse cultural backgrounds build understanding of oneself, the communities within which the learner lives, and the world.

What Is Influencing Best Practices in Curriculum, Instruction, and Assessment in Language Classrooms Today?

Certainly, past practice influences how we are teaching languages today. Over the years, languages have been taught in ways that conformed to the most recent theory of how a language should be taught. Teachers adapted their practices to the best information that was available at the time, often recognizing that the method of instruction did not address the diverse intelligences and learning styles of all learners. Appendix C summarizes selected theories, methods, and approaches, and offers a brief example of language that learners might produce as the result of each method. Many of today's classrooms utilize a combination of these theories, methods, and approaches.

Over the last decade, much has changed in what we know about teaching and learning. Advances in neuroscience have informed what we understand about how learning takes place. Technology has made it possible to reinvent the learning environment in ways that expand the opportunities learners have for collaboration and communication with people around the world. Teachers are challenged to incorporate 21st Century Skills and the Common Core State Standards into instructional units based on the Standards for Learning Languages. In order to bring coherence to these influences, we propose that curriculum, unit, and lesson design for language learning consider three key factors:

- what we teach;
- how we teach; and
- how we know that students have learned.

For many, the discussion about what we teach (curriculum), how we teach (instruction), and how we know that students have learned (assessment) will validate what is already common practice in their classrooms. Some may find that they want to make adjustments to allow for increased alignment with the Standards for Learning Languages, 21st Century Skills, and/or Common Core State Standards. For others these concepts may trigger a paradigm shift, a realization that the current curriculum used in their school or district is not sufficient to develop the skills that today's learners need.

How Do the Standards for Learning Languages Facilitate Curriculum, Unit, and Lesson Design?

The Standards for Learning Languages. *Standards for Foreign Language Learning* (National Standards in Foreign Language Education Project [NSFLEP], 1996) was first published in 1996, and united the profession around what learners should know and be able to do in order to understand and communicate in a language other than English. The Standards define five goal areas, the 5 Cs—Communication, Cultures, Connections, Comparisons, and Communities—and 11 standards for those goal areas. *"Knowing how, when and why to say what to whom"* (NSFLEP, 2006, p. 11), captures the vision of what it means to communicate in a language other than English. The Communication goal area goes beyond the "what" (vocabulary) and the "how" (grammar), expanding to a more complete definition of communication indicating "why" (the purpose), "when" (the time and place), and with or to "whom" (the audience). The Standards give the profession a way of explaining that grammar and vocabulary are tools for learning a language, but that proficiency in another language requires the ability to communicate in meaningful and appropriate ways with other speakers of that language. Because of the Standards, language learning is no longer limited to what learners know *about* the language, but focuses on what they can do *with* the language. Today, the profession recognizes the visionary work done by those who developed the Standards in 1996. When they were first created, the 5 Cs offered a simple yet cohesive way to frame language learning. Over time, the complexity and richness of the Standards became apparent to those who used them to guide their work. The Standards align to both the 21st Century Skills and the Common Core State Standards, highlighting the importance and value of language study in meeting these cross-disciplinary initiatives to prepare young people for advanced studies, work, careers, and active participation in today's global community.

Let's consider the Standards in the context of a thematic unit on "Challenges" related to the topic of education at the Novice High/Intermediate Low level of proficiency. Table 1 presents a brief overview to a unit about the importance of education for all young people. The complete education unit can be found in Appendix D and at www.actfl.org/publications/books-and-bro-chures/the-keys-planning-learning. Learners explore the topic of education on a personal level (*Knowing Myself*), in their local communities (*Exploring Communities*), and globally (*Engaging with the World*). Throughout the unit the learners will explore possible responses to the essential question: "Why can't all children go to school?" The goals reflect what learners should know and be able to do by the end of the unit.

Table 1. Overview to Thematic Unit on Education

Language and Level/Grade	French – Novice High ➔ Intermediate Low
Theme/Topic	**Challenges:** Education
Essential Question	Why can't all children go to school?
Goals *What should learners know and be able to do by the end of the unit?*	Learners will be able to: • describe the current status of education of young people locally, nationally, and globally • identify and categorize economic, political, and social reasons why young people around the world cannot go to/stay in school • give reasons why going to school is important to oneself and locally, nationally, globally • give examples of initiatives to support schooling for all young people around the world • connect with a school in (x) to learn more about the school; collaborate to develop a plan for continued communication

Now, let's consider how the 5 Cs—Communication, Cultures, Connections, Comparisons and Communities—are integrated within this unit.

GOAL AREA: COMMUNICATION – Communicate effectively in more than one language in order to function in a variety of situations and for multiple purposes.

The Communication goal area includes three standards representing the three modes of communication:

- **Interpersonal Communication:** Learners participate in unrehearsed spoken, signed, and written conversations, exchanging information, ideas, opinions, and feelings, and reacting/responding to information, ideas, opinions, and feelings expressed by others.

- **Interpretive Communication:** Learners read, listen to, and view both informational (non-fiction) and literary (fiction) texts, demonstrating understanding of the literal and inferred meanings.

- **Presentational Communication:** Learners present information, concepts, and ideas that have been rehearsed or edited to an audience of listeners or readers, using technology as appropriate to the purpose of the presentation.

In order to meet the Communication goals for this unit, learners work with a variety of authentic texts in the interpretive mode to learn more about why all children can't go to school. Based on what they learn, they design a multimedia campaign to inform others about education around the world in the presentational mode. Finally, in the interpersonal mode, they discuss with others what they have learned in order to address the unit's essential question of why all children can't go to school. Table 2 summarizes the summative performance assessment for the unit. Note that all three modes are represented in the summative assessment.

Table 2. Summative Performance Assessment for Thematic Unit on Education

Mode	Learners will:
Interpretive	• view a video about education in Sénégal • read and view information published by UNICEF on the rights of the child to an education • read an article on the importance of school
Presentational	• work collaboratively to design a multimedia campaign about education around the world and involve others in the campaign
Interpersonal	• discuss with peers reasons why children around the world can't go to school including reasons why education is essential

GOAL AREA: CULTURES – Interact with cultural competence and understanding.

The Cultures goal area includes two standards connecting practices and products of the culture to underlying perspectives:

• **Relating Cultural Practices to Perspectives:** Demonstrate an understanding of the relationship between cultural practices and perspectives of the cultures. Practices include behaviors such as how people greet each other, what people do on weekends, and how people show respect.

• **Relating Cultural Products to Perspectives:** Demonstrate an understanding of the relationship between the cultural products and perspectives of the cultures. Products refer to objects such as paintings, monuments, music, and literature.

The Cultures goal area is often referred to as the 3 Ps (products, practices, perspectives) and a triangle is used to illustrate the relationship of a practice to a product and the underlying perspective (Figure 2).

Figure 2. Culture Triangle

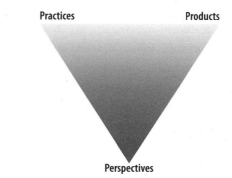

In the education unit, learners consider school as a *product* of the culture, and going to school in a particular country as a *practice* of the culture. The *perspectives* based on attending school reflect the value a culture places on education for its youth. Learners might also look at daily class schedules (*products*) for an understanding of required and elective courses (*practices*), and consider what the product and practices imply about the purpose of education in that culture (*perspectives*). Table 3 shows the Cultures goal area as it appears in the unit template.

Table 3. Cultures Goal Area Represented in the Thematic Unit on Education

Cultures (Sample Evidence) *Indicate the relationship between the product, practice, and perspective.*	**Product:** School **Practice:** Going to school **Perspective:** Importance of school for all young people in (x) **Product:** Daily class schedule **Practice:** Required vs. elective courses **Perspective:** Purpose of school

GOAL AREA: CONNECTIONS – Connect with other disciplines and acquire information and diverse perspectives in order to use the language to function in academic and career-related situations.

The Connections goal area includes two standards that emphasize how learners are able to build content knowledge by relating what they are learning in their language class to other disciplines.

• **Making Connections:** Learners reinforce and expand their knowledge of other disciplines through the language they are learning.

• **Acquiring Information and Diverse Perspectives:** Learners acquire information and recognize distinctive viewpoints through the language and its culture.

In the education unit, learners work with authentic texts that convey information about the basic right of a child to an education. They consider literacy rates around the world and read the opinions of others to understand why participation rates in schooling vary across cultures, connecting to content they might discuss in a social studies course. They use their language skills to support and defend their ideas drawing on the evidence in texts in the target language to support their opinions, addressing the English Language Arts Common Core Writing Anchor Standard 1: "Write arguments to support claims in an analysis of substantive topics or texts using valid reasoning and relevant and sufficient evidence" (www.corestandards.org). At first glance, this Common Core Standard may seem out of reach for novice language learners. However, if the learners have the opportunity to interact with several authentic texts in a guided process, they can achieve this standard. For example, in the thematic unit on education, learners may have brainstormed why they think all children around the world cannot go to school. Their next task is to read articles on the Internet about the topic, looking at headlines and introductory paragraphs to see what issues related to school attendance are addressed. They can then list the issues presented in the authentic texts to support their claims about why all children cannot go to school. Table 4 shows the Connections goal area as it appears in the unit template.

Table 4. Connections Goal Area Represented in the Thematic Unit on Education

Connections (Sample Evidence)	Making Connections	Acquiring Information and Diverse Perspectives
	Social Studies: • Education as a right of the child (United Nations) • Global challenge of educating all young people **English Language Arts:** • Synthesis of information from a variety of sources • Sharing information and ideas with others through discussions	Education systems and practices around the world and reasons for those systems and practices

GOAL AREA: COMPARISONS – Develop insight into the nature of language and culture in order to interact with cultural competence.

The Comparisons goal area includes two standards that encourage learners to compare the language and culture they are studying to their own.

- **Language Comparisons:** Compare the language learners are studying to their own
- **Cultural Comparisons:** Compare the culture learners are studying to their own

In the education unit, learners explore the concept of *une année blanche* (literally, a white year) considering how another culture and language convey a missed year of schooling. Learners make comparisons to their own lives by exploring reasons that their educational year might be disrupted. They consider the implications of passing or failing the *bac*, the exam given at the end of high school in Francophone countries, in comparison to the impact of exams given in the United States. They recognize that *passer* is a false cognate in the phrase *passer le bac* and means "to take the *bac*" and not "to get a passing grade on the *bac*." Table 5 shows the Comparisons goal area as it appears in the unit template.

Table 5. Comparisons Goal Area Represented in the Thematic Unit on Education

Comparisons (Sample Evidence)	Language Comparisons	Cultural Comparisons
	• *une année blanche* (a missed year) • *passer le bac* (to take the *bac*)	• Reasons to attend/not attend school • Exams in high school

GOAL AREA: COMMUNITIES – Communicate and interact with cultural competence in order to participate in multilingual communities at home and around the world.

The Communities goal area includes two standards and recognizes the need for learners to communicate with other speakers of the language while taking personal responsibility for their own learning.

- **School and Global Communities:** Use the language both within and beyond the school setting
- **Lifelong Learning:** Show evidence of becoming lifelong learners by using the language for personal enjoyment, enrichment, and career advancement.

In the presentational task for the unit on education, learners prepare a multimedia campaign to inform people in the community about school attendance around the world. Learners may continue to monitor this issue independently after completing the unit in class. Discussions in class during this unit about the importance of school may influence learners to set personal goals related to their plans for continuing their education after high school. Table 6 shows the Communities goal area as it appears in the unit template.

Table 6. Communities Goal Area Represented in the Thematic Unit on Education

Communities (Sample Evidence)	School and Global Communities	Lifelong Learning
	Inform others about education around the world and opportunities for collaboration on a project related to education for all.	Consider the role that education plays in your life and set personal goals.

The 5 Cs—Communication, Cultures, Connections, Comparisons, Communities—guide the choice of content for a curriculum designed to build proficiency in the three modes of Communication *embedded in a cultural context*, and enriched by Comparisons, Connections, and Communities.

> Language-specific Standards are currently available in Arabic, American Sign Language (ASL), Chinese, Classical Languages, French, German, Hindi, Italian, Japanese, Korean, Portuguese, Russian, Scandinavian Languages, and Spanish. www.actfl.org/publications/all/national-standards-foreign-language-education

What Other Resources Facilitate Curriculum, Unit, and Lesson Design?

ACTFL Proficiency Guidelines. The *ACTFL Proficiency Guidelines* were first published in 1986 and most recently revised in 2012. They assess how well a person uses language independent of how they learned that language (see Appendix B). They explain "what individuals can do with language in terms of speaking, writing, listening, and reading in real-world situations in a spontaneous and non-rehearsed context" (ACTFL, 2012a). They include descriptions of proficiency at the Novice, Intermediate, Advanced, Superior, and Distinguished levels.

> The complete *ACTFL Proficiency Guidelines* are located at actflproficiencyguidelines2012.org.

ACTFL Performance Descriptors for Language Learners. First released as the *ACTFL Performance Guidelines for K–12 Learners* in 1998, they were updated and released in 2012 as the *ACTFL Performance Descriptors for Language Learners* (ACTFL, 2012b) (see Appendix E). The Standards for Learning Languages describe what learners should know and be able to do. The performance descriptors indicate how well a learner should perform at Novice, Intermediate, and Advanced ranges of performance for each mode of communication based on what has been learned and practiced in the classroom. It is important to note that, in the classroom setting, learners are likely to perform better than they would in a proficiency (real-world) situation. This is because in the classroom, the contexts and topics for performance are familiar and practiced. Outside the classroom, the contexts and topics are not limited to what has been taught. Consider how Figure 3 depicts the differences between performance and proficiency.

Figure 3. Contexts for Performance and Proficiency

Performance	Proficiency
Based on instruction; familiar content	Independent of instruction; broad content

When learners are in a school setting, they are working with language in the context of a specific unit, where the language being studied is more constrained and more predictable, with the learning being scaffolded by a supportive and knowledgeable teacher. The school image captures performance, what learners do based on instruction. As they continue to study the language, they are increasingly well-prepared to use that language outside of the classroom. The image of the Eiffel Tower reflects proficiency, what learners can do when they are using language in unrehearsed, less predictable situations outside the classroom with people who do not know what topics the learner is currently studying.

The *ACTFL Performance Descriptors for Language Learners* are located at www.actfl.org/publications/ guidelines-and-manuals/actfl-performance-descriptors-language-learners.

NCSSFL LinguaFolio® and NCSSFL-ACTFL Can-Do Statements. The National Council of State Supervisors for Languages (NCSSFL) LinguaFolio® is based on the European Language Portfolio (ELP), the Standards for Learning Languages, the 1998 ACTFL Performance Guidelines, and the ACTFL Proficiency Guidelines (see Appendix B). Originally developed by members of NCSSFL, LinguaFolio is a standards-based, formative assessment tool where learners can document their language learning progress and their growth in interculturality. More information on LinguaFolio follows in the next section. NCSSFL and ACTFL collaborated to refine the statements of what the learner can do to demonstrate performance that points toward each specific proficiency level. The resulting document, *NCSSFL-ACTFL Can-Do Statements*, is useful in identifying appropriate learning activities and performance tasks.

Table 7 summarizes the key characteristics of these three resources designed to facilitate curriculum, instruction, and assessment in the world language classroom.

How Can the 4 Cs—Communication, Critical Thinking and Problem Solving, Creativity and Innovation, Collaboration and Cross-Cultural Understanding—of the 21st Century Skills Facilitate Language Instruction?

Instructional Repertoire. The 5 Cs of the Standards for Learning Languages—Communication, Cultures, Connections, Comparisons, and Communities—guide the choice of content to build linguistic and cultural proficiency in languages other than English. In addition to the 5 Cs, we have chosen the 4 Cs of the 21st Century Skills—Communication, Critical Thinking and Problem Solving, Creativity and Innovation, Collaboration and Cross-Cultural Understanding—to organize a language teacher's Instructional Repertoire. By Instructional Repertoire, we mean all the tools teachers use to facilitate learning

Table 7. Relationships Among the ACTFL Proficiency Guidelines, NCSSFL-ACTFL Can-Do Statements, and ACTFL Performance Descriptors

	ACTFL Proficiency Guidelines	**NCSSFL-ACTFL Can-Do Statements**	**ACTFL Performance Descriptors for Language Learners**
Purpose	Describes what language learners can do regardless of how the language was acquired	States what learners can do specific to each communication mode and level of proficiency	Describes what language learners can do based on instruction in an academic setting
Communication Skills	Speaking Listening Reading Writing	Interpersonal Interpretive Presentational	Interpersonal Interpretive Presentational
Levels	Novice Intermediate Advanced Superior Distinguished	Novice Intermediate Advanced Superior Distinguished	Novice Intermediate Advanced
Contexts	Unrehearsed Broad	Customized/Personalized to Individual Goals	Practiced Familiar
Considerations	Content Context Accuracy Discourse Type	Self-assessment (e.g., I can do this, I can do this with help, I am still practicing)	Functions Contexts/Content Text Type Language Control Vocabulary Communication Strategies Cultural Awareness

Figure 4. Instructional Repertoire for Language Teachers

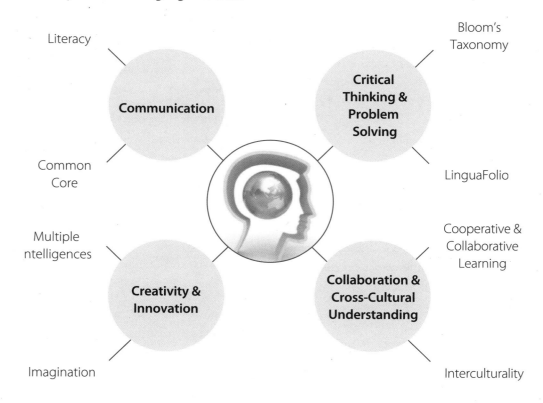

for the increasingly diverse population of learners in language classrooms. Instead of describing a long list of instructional tools, we have highlighted ones that suggest meaningful ways to build communication skills and interculturality while at the same time developing 21st century skills. Teachers are encouraged to share components from this framework with learners to promote their growth and independence in taking more responsibility for their learning. Figure 4 represents the components of the Instructional Repertoire.

In the organizational framework for the Instructional Repertoire, the learner is in the center as a reminder that each learner has unique needs and interests, requiring differentiation of instruction for successful language learning. Placing the learner in the center also indicates that the learner can use these instructional tools to build 21st century skills, and become an independent learner. The imprint of the world on the mind of the learner highlights the connection between 21st century skills and the development of interculturality.

For more information on the Partnership for 21st Century Skills, visit www.p21.org.

For more information on the World Languages 21st Skills Map, visit www.p21.org/storage/documents/Skills%20Map/ p21_worldlanguagesmap.pdf.

Each of the 4 Cs of the 21st Century Skills—Communication, Critical Thinking, Creativity, and Collaboration—is presented individually in this section. However, it is important to remember that these skills are interconnected with overlapping characteristics and real-world applications. Following a brief explanation of each C of the 21st Century Skills, suggestions for application of each skill in the world language classroom are presented. These classroom applications, while directly connected to one of the Cs of the 21st Century Skills, are tools that learners can use to develop all 4 Cs of the 21st Century Skills. As you read the descriptions of the 21st Century Skills, you may be reminded of the Common Core State Standards for English Language Arts. The 21st Century Skills complement Common Core State Standards. Combined with the Standards for Learning Languages, these initiatives create a strong foundation of knowledge and skills needed for success in work and life in the 21st century.

Communication. Being an effective communicator in the 21st century requires more skills than simply being able to read and write. Recognizing the changes in society and technology in today's world, the National Council of Teachers of English (NCTE) has expanded the definition of literacy to address the intensity and complexity of a rapidly changing world. Their definition of 21st century literacy (NCTE, 2013) states:

Active, successful participants in this 21st century global society must be able to:
- develop proficiency and fluency with the tools of technology;
- build intentional cross-cultural connections and relationships with others so to pose and solve problems collaboratively and strengthen independent thought;
- design and share information for global communities to meet a variety of purposes;
- manage, analyze, and synthesize multiple streams of simultaneous information;
- create, critique, analyze, and evaluate multimedia texts; and
- attend to the ethical responsibilities required by these complex environments.

The Partnership for 21st Century Skills devotes an entire portion of the Skills Framework for 21st Century Learning to Information Literacy, Media Literacy, and Information and Communication Technology (ICT) Literacy. The NCTE definition of 21st century literacy and the Partnership for 21st Century Skills both emphasize the effective use of print and digital media to build communication skills both as a consumer and as a producer of information in a global context. Successful communication in the 21st century includes the following skills:
- expressing thoughts and ideas clearly and effectively in a variety of oral and written forms and contexts for a variety of purposes and for a variety of audiences;
- listening and reading to decipher literal meaning and inferences; and
- using and interpreting a variety of media and technologies, judging their effectiveness and impact in communicating a message (www.p21.org/overview/skills-framework/261).

The Common Core State Standards for English Language Arts underline the importance of these literacy skills among learn-

ers. "With today's and tomorrow's digital tools, our net generation students will have unprecedented power to amplify their ability to think, learn, communicate, collaborate, and create" (Trilling & Fadel, 2009, p. 61). The next sections show how 21st century communication skills are reinforced through the three modes of communication.

Building Literacy Through the Interpersonal Mode. The Interpersonal Mode is two-way communication where the learners exchange ideas and information. While interpersonal communication occurs most often via conversations, online exchanges of information, such as e-mails or texting, are also considered to be interpersonal. Language learners can build literacy skills via the interpersonal mode by:
- exchanging ideas and information purposefully and with clarity;
- listening attentively to what participants in discussions and conversations say;
- engaging other participants by inviting their perspectives on the topic;
- monitoring the participants in a conversation to see if they understand the message, clarifying and elaborating as appropriate;
- withholding judgment during the exchange of ideas and information;
- evaluating what others say in terms of logical reasoning and evidence;
- using follow-up questions and comments to clarify and expand on the topic; and
- adjusting nonverbal and verbal communication to the cultural context of the conversation.

All of these behaviors can be encouraged among language learners by incorporating them into scoring guides. For example, in addition to assessing use of vocabulary and comprehensibility, teachers could also add categories such as evidence of active listening or use of follow-up questions and comments to give learners ideas on how to be a good participant in a discussion or conversation.

The Common Core State Standards for Speaking and Listening emphasize collaboration. In the Common Core Anchor Standards, those end goals representing what students graduating from high school in the United States should know and be able to do, collaboration in speaking and listening is described as Standard 1 (SL1): "Prepare for and participate effectively in a range of conversations and collaborations with diverse partners, building on others' ideas and expressing their own clearly and persuasively" (www.corestandards.org). Examples of situations requiring these interpersonal skills are listed below and can be accomplished via technology including tools such as Skype, e-mail, avatars, discussion boards, and videoconferencing to connect learners in your classroom with learners in classrooms in other places, locally, nationally, and internationally. Learners can:

- carry on a conversation about daily life and events;
- make plans (to meet someone, attend an event, to travel somewhere, host a videoconference, etc.);
- ask and respond to questions about a topic being studied in class;
- compare reactions to something or someone from pop culture;
- share insights gained from a movie or piece of literature;
- work with others to design and complete a task or project;
- express and compare opinions and preferences about topics of interest; and
- participate in a panel discussion or debate on a topic currently in the news.

Building Literacy Through the Presentational Mode. The Presentational Mode is one-way communication via speaking or writing where the learners present ideas and information that they have rehearsed and polished for an audience. Learners can build their literacy through presentational skills by:

- documenting ideas from a brainstorming session via a graphic organizer;
- using an outline to organize ideas and information for the presentation;
- planning and editing to produce a clear, organized, and informative presentation;
- demonstrating that, through choice of vocabulary, register, and topic, the learner is aware of the audience for the presentation;
- summarizing the main idea and supporting details from a variety of sources;
- synthesizing information from several sources to present a new perspective on a topic;
- using evidence-based reasoning and arguments to support an opinion; and
- using technology appropriately to enhance understanding of the presentation.

Tasks can be presented or enhanced via technology to create products such as wikis, videos, webpages, blogs, podcasts, and timelines. Examples of presentational tasks include:

- stories based on past experiences, real or imagined;
- cartoon strips illustrating an original story;
- news stories based on a current event;
- demonstrations of how to do something through a speech or through written instructions;
- brochures, leaflets, and flyers on a person, place, or event of interest;
- podcasts on a person, place, or event of interest;
- videos or live performances of an original script;
- persuasive speeches or essays on a topic of importance locally, nationally, or internationally;
- researched reports based on findings from multiple sources; and
- websites or blogs on a person, place, or event of interest.

The tasks listed above address the Common Core Writing and Speaking Standards. The Writing Standards require learners to write arguments, informative and explanatory texts including research papers, and narratives. The writing must be clear and coherent. Learners need to use the writing process to plan, revise, edit, rewrite their texts. They must use technology to produce and share their writing and oral presentations with others. Finally, learners must demonstrate that they can write over both short and extended time frames, and prepare oral presentations for a range of tasks, purposes, and audiences (www.corestandards.org).

Building Literacy Through the Interpretive Mode. The Interpretive Mode is one-way communication via listening, reading, or viewing where the learners take in ideas and information from a wide variety of print and digital media. Learners can build their literacy through interpretive skills by using pre-reading strategies/pre-listening or viewing strategies in preparation for reading, listening to, or viewing the text. Learners will be more successful at interpreting text when they:

- preview the type of text (e.g., newspaper, magazine, short story, news broadcast, song, or movie);
- preview the title and any visuals to begin to form ideas about the content;
- check the sources for the text to see if they are credible;
- with a partner, list what is known about the topic and then make predictions about what the text is about;

- for written texts, read the first and last paragraphs of the text, make revisions to predictions as appropriate; and
- share with classmates predictions about the text.

To build literacy in reading:
- note main idea of each paragraph in the margin;
- note connections of the ideas in the text to other texts or experiences;
- write a question or questions about the information presented on the page;
- underline words that are important to understanding the meaning of the text: try to limit the number of words underlined to words that are essential to understanding the text; and
- reread text after defining underlined words to gain deeper understanding of the text.

To build literacy when viewing a video clip:
- view the clip without sound the first time, making predictions about the content;
- view the clip with sound to modify predictions, add information;
- note images that are especially helpful and/or memorable in understanding the commentary; and
- note background sounds and music and how they facilitate understanding the message(s).

To analyze the text after reading, listening, or viewing:
- draw the main ideas and supporting details from a text to demonstrate understanding;
- create a timeline of events in the text;
- use graphic organizers to outline the main ideas and supporting details of a text;
- discuss the surface purpose for the text and writer's motivations;
- take what was learned from the text and draw conclusions that are not directly stated in the text but can be inferred; and
- conduct a Socratic seminar to analyze, synthesize, and evaluate points of view presented in the text.

It is important that teachers use multiple authentic texts to build learners' literacy skills. Authentic texts are "those written and oral communications produced by members of a language and culture group for members of the same language and culture group" (Shrum & Glisan, 2010, p. 85). Shrum and Glisan acknowledge that texts may contain vocabulary and structures that learners have not studied but state that the real

difficulty is in the task that learners are asked to complete, not in the text itself. They recommend following the suggestion: "Edit the task, not the text" (Shrum & Glisan, 2010, p. 88). For example, look at the front page of a newspaper. Novice learners might be asked to identify the places where the front page stories take place. Intermediate learners might be asked to list the topics presented on the front page of the newspaper. Advanced learners might read the front page of the newspaper for content, and then analyze why the press featured the articles on the front page.

The Interpretive Mode of Communication supports the Common Core Reading Standards. Common Core encourages learners to interact with a balance of both fiction and nonfiction texts, with texts selected from a broad range of cultures and periods. Common Core also recommends that learners interact with increasingly complex texts over time in order to build proficiency (www.corestandards.org).

Critical Thinking and Problem Solving. Many leaders in business, education, and government advocate for the development of critical thinking skills as a fundamental goal of education. In 1941, Glaser in *An Experiment in the Development of Critical Thinking* (1972) stated that critical thinking required examining beliefs and supposed facts through the lens of evidence. In language classrooms that integrate 21st century skills, the opportunity is available for learners to use language purposefully to explore real-world topics of interest and importance. Learners can interact with a variety of authentic texts to gather evidence that supports their understanding of the people who speak the language they are learning and their related culture. The ongoing challenge for language teachers is how to develop critical thinking skills in learners who are operating linguistically at the Novice and Intermediate levels of proficiency.

Consider how the Partnership for 21st Century Skills describes the characteristics of learners who are critical thinkers and problem-solvers (www.p21.org). These learners:
- reason effectively;
- identify and analyze systems and patterns;
- evaluate and analyze a variety of points of view and evidence;
- synthesize and interpret information from multiple sources;
- propose new ways to solve problems;
- ask important questions to clarify points of view and promote deeper thinking; and
- reflect critically on learning experiences.

In designing classroom instruction, Bloom's Taxonomy (Bloom, 1956) is an extremely helpful reference tool that gives examples of how to move from the lower order thinking skills of remembering, understanding, and applying to the higher level skills of analyzing, evaluating, and creating. In a language classroom, learners often spend a significant amount of time remembering and understanding the target language. When teachers actively apply Bloom's Taxonomy, learners have the opportunity to apply the language they have learned to a variety of tasks and situations, to analyze and evaluate situations where the language is used, and ultimately to create a product that uses the language that they have learned.

A second tool that is useful in developing critical thinking is the LinguaFolio and the NCSSFL-ACTFL Can-Do Statements (www.actfl.org/publications/guidelines-and-manuals/can-do-statements). LinguaFolio is a portfolio designed to help learners set personal goals for learning a language, and then self-assess their progress towards achieving their goals. The Can-Do Statements are based on the 2012 ACTFL Proficiency Guidelines, providing descriptors of performance in the three modes of communication in terms of what learners can do at the Novice, Intermediate, Advanced, Superior, and Distinguished levels of proficiency. LinguaFolio also includes guide questions to help learners reflect on their interactions with other cultures. What follows is a discussion of the classroom applications for Bloom's Taxonomy and LinguaFolio. As you read, imagine how Bloom's Taxonomy and the Can-Do Statements could be integrated into your lesson and unit plans.

Bloom's Taxonomy. Bloom's Taxonomy, originally published in 1956 by a group of educational psychologists including Benjamin Bloom, was developed as a classification system of question types for professors to reference in order to encourage their use of higher-level questions designed to increase learning. In 2001 Loren Anderson, a former student of Benjamin Bloom, led a group of cognitive psychologists, curriculum theorists, and instructional researchers in the revision of the Taxonomy to reflect advances in learning theory and practices. The revised taxonomy used verbs instead of nouns to show learners' thinking processes, and moves from lower order thinking skills (remembering, understanding, applying) to higher order thinking skills (analyzing, evaluating, creating). Figure 5 shows the levels of Bloom's Revised Taxonomy (Anderson, Krahthwohl, & Bloom, 2001).

Figure 5. Bloom's Revised Taxonomy (2001)

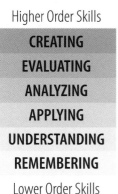

Higher Order Skills

CREATING
EVALUATING
ANALYZING
APPLYING
UNDERSTANDING
REMEMBERING

Lower Order Skills

Table 8 shows the levels of Bloom's Revised Taxonomy, and includes action verbs associated with each level and sample learning activities for the language classroom. The italicized words in the sample learning activities column reflect suggestions for digital alternatives as proposed by Andrew Churches, a classroom teacher in Auckland, New Zealand, and a co-author of several books on the role of technology in the 21st century classroom.

Table 8. Bloom's Revised Taxonomy
(Adapted from Andrew Churches's Bloom's Digital Taxonomy, edorigami.wikispaces.com)

Classification	Action Verbs	Sample Learning Activities
Remembering: Can the learner recall or remember previously learned information?	Define Describe Find Identify List Locate Match Memorize Name Recall Recite Recognize Record Relate Repeat Reproduce State Tell Underline	• Exchange greetings and ask simple memorized questions • Identify historic places in (city, country) • Label a picture, image • Make a timeline • Match an image to the written word • Name (places in the city) • Underline words that describe (x) **Digital alternatives** • *Bookmark* • *Highlight* • *List using bullet points* • *Search*
Understanding: Can the learner explain or restate ideas and concepts?	Choose Cite examples of… Clarify Classify Compare Demonstrate the use of… Describe Discuss Explain Express Illustrate Infer Interpret Outline Paraphrase Predict Report Restate Summarize Tell about…	• Compare (school schedules) in the target culture with those in the U.S. • Complete a graphic organizer • Illustrate the main idea(s) • Make inferences about a text based on knowledge of target culture • Predict what a text is about based on visuals, title of the text • Retell a story that was heard or read or viewed **Digital alternatives** • *Annotate* • *Blog* • *Categorize* • *Comment* • *Conduct advanced searches* • *Tag* • *Tweet*

Table 8. Bloom's Revised Taxonomy (continued)
(Adapted from Andrew Churches's Bloom's Digital Taxonomy, edorigami.wikispaces.com)

Classification	Action Verbs	Sample Learning Activities
Applying: Can the learner use what was learned in a new way or situation such as a presentation, simulation, or interview?	Apply Change Choose Construct Demonstrate Dramatize Edit Experiment Illustrate Implement Interview Make Modify Perform Present Produce Put into practice Share Solve Use	• Dramatize a day in the life of a student in the target culture • Interview someone who has traveled or lived in the target culture • Make a presentation about (traveling respectfully) • Proofread a text • Suggest ways to collaborate with a school in the target culture **Digital alternatives** • *Blog* • *Chat* • *Edit using online tools* • *Podcast* • *Skype* • *Text* • *Upload a presentation* • *Use PowerPoint* • *Videoconference* • *Vodcast*
Analyzing: Can the learner break information into parts and show the relationships among the parts?	Analyze Calculate Categorize Compare Conclude Contrast Correlate Critique Debate Deconstruct Detect Diagram Evaluate Examine Integrate Organize Outline Question Subdivide	• Categorize lifestyle influences based on where one lives • Contrast the importance of family in the target culture to the U.S. • Correlate cultural products to practices and perspectives • Design a questionnaire about (x) and analyze the results **Digital alternatives** • *Diagram* • *Graphic organizer* • *Link* • *Mash* • *Online polls and surveys* • *Venn diagram*

Table 8. Bloom's Revised Taxonomy (continued)
(Adapted from Andrew Churches's Bloom's Digital Taxonomy, edorigami.wikispaces.com)

Classification	Action Verbs	Sample Learning Activities
Evaluating: Can the learner justify an opinion or judge the worth of information based on standards and criteria?	Assess Choose Critique Defend Determine Evaluate Judge Justify Rate Reflect Test Validate Weigh	• Debate an issue that is in the news • Design a rubric to evaluate a project • Keep a reflective journal about cultural encounters and your responses in those encounters • Rate an oral presentation • Self-assess language learning progress • Write an editorial **Digital alternatives** • *Blog* • *Chatrooms* • *Comments* • *Discussion board* • *Moderated thread* • *Posts* • *Reviews* • *Threaded discussion* • *Wiki*
Creating: Can the learner put together separate ideas or information to create a new product or point of view?	Assemble Compose Construct Create Design Develop Devise Hypothesize Imagine Invent Make Modify Plan Prepare Produce Propose	• Create a modern-day version of a classic story • Design a website for a language class • Imagine time traveling back to an historic event **Digital alternatives** • *Animation* • *Blog* • *Broadcast* • *Digital stories* • *Film* • *Online publishing* • *Podcast*

The list of action verbs along with the sample activities in Table 8 are organized from lower order to higher order thinking skills. When planning units and daily lessons, language teachers should utilize the full range of action verbs and suggested activities to facilitate learning. Novice language learners are as capable as Intermediate and Advanced language learners of analyzing, evaluating, and creating using the target language. For example, in a thematic unit about living in a city, Novice-level learners could:

- **locate** places in a city on a map of the city (*Remembering*);
- **compare** places in a city in (x) to those in the learner's city (*Understanding*);
- **dramatize** a day in the city of (x) (*Applying*);
- **categorize** places in the city that provide services and those that are businesses (*Analyzing*);
- **choose** places in a city in (x) and in the learner's city that make the cities special (*Evaluating*); and
- **design** a poster that highlights places in city (x) (*Creating*).

Not only is Bloom's Taxonomy useful in planning cognitively engaging lessons, it is also a helpful reference in selecting vocabulary that learners need in order to actively participate in selected activities such as those described above. For example, in order for learners to categorize places in a city that provide services and those that are businesses, they would need vocabulary to name and describe places that provide services such as "library," "fire department," "police department," and "city hall." They would also need vocabulary that would allow them to name and describe businesses such as "grocery store," "pharmacy," and "coffee shop."

LinguaFolio. Reflection and goal setting are designed to build and solidify learning while encouraging learners to be self-regulated and independent. LinguaFolio is a portfolio designed to help learners self-assess their progress in understanding and using a language. Designed to demystify the process of learning another language, LinguaFolio includes broad Can-Do Statements in the three modes of communication across five levels of proficiency (Novice, Intermediate, Advanced, Superior, and Distinguished). Based on these broad statements of what learners can do in each of the modes of communication at various levels of proficiency, learners can set communication goals that are personalized to the topics they are exploring. During the unit of instruction, learners can self-assess their progress towards reaching those goals.

Research conducted by Ziegler and Moeller (2012) suggests that LinguaFolio increases self-regulated learning in students. When teachers use LinguaFolio extensively, learners increase their accuracy in self-assessment, and in achieving the goals they set. Ziegler and Moeller noted that regular integration of goal writing followed by reflection on the evidence of achievement of those goals was important to the success of LinguaFolio. ACTFL collaborated with the NCSSFL in 2013 to update the design and contents of LinguaFolio's Can-Do Statements. The NCSSFL-ACTFL Can-Do Statements are available at: www.actfl.org/publications/guidelines-and-manuals/can-do-statements.

To implement LinguaFolio in the classroom, the first step in introducing a new unit of instruction is to share with learners the overarching goals for the unit: What will the learners know and be able to do at the end of the unit of instruction? These overarching goals related to the unit's essential question can be presented in the form of Can-Do Statements, and posted for reference throughout the teaching of the unit. For example, in the sample unit A Balanced Lifestyle presented in detail in Chapter 2, the essential question is: How do people here and in (the French-speaking world) describe a balanced lifestyle? The Can-Do Statements for the unit include:

- I can explore health and wellness websites to identify elements of a balanced lifestyle here and in (country in the French-speaking world);
- I can compare lifestyles of teenagers to those of teenagers in (country in the French-speaking world) in terms of balance;
- I can make recommendations for ways to create or maintain a balanced lifestyle; and
- I can create a presentation for (the community) highlighting ways to promote a balanced lifestyle.

All of these overarching Can-Do Statements respond to different aspects of the essential question. Cultural products and practices are embedded in the Can-Do Statements to ensure that cultural perspectives related to those products and practices are explored.

Each day of the unit, the teacher posts Can-Do Statements that are specific to that day's instruction. For example, one lesson in the balanced lifestyle unit focuses on using the vocabulary related to daily exercise and applies the linguistic function of frequency, both learned in prior lessons. The Can-Do Statements for this lesson include:

- I can ask and respond to questions about physical activities that people my age do and how often they do these activities;
- I can compare the physical activities that people my age do in the U.S. and compare them to activities that people my age do in (x); and
- I can categorize physical activities that people my age do in terms of how they contribute to physical fitness.

The LinguaFolio portfolio includes space for learners to write specific Can-Do Statements for each mode of communication. Table 9 shows the broad Can-Do Statement and the specific Can-Do Statement for the unit on a balanced lifestyle.

Table 9. LinguaFolio Examples of Can-Do Statements for Novice High Learners

Mode	Broad Can-Do Statements	Specific Can-Do Statements
Interpersonal	I can exchange some personal information.	I can ask and respond to questions about physical activities that people my age do and how often they do these activities.
Presentational Writing	I can write information about my daily life.	I can compare the physical activities that people my age do in the U.S. with activities that people my age do in (x) in a class blog.
Presentational Writing	I can write basic information about things I have learned.	I can categorize physical activities that people my age do in terms of how they contribute to physical fitness in a class blog.

LinguaFolio begins as a partnership between the teacher and the learner in determining how the instructional goals for a unit will be met. As learners become familiar with LinguaFolio and the goal setting process, they create their own Can-Do Statements for a unit of study, identifying what they want to learn and to be able to do related to the unit theme. This process encourages learners to critically reflect on what they are learning and how they are learning, contributing to their development as independent learners. Ultimately, they set personal goals for what they want to know and be able to do related to building communicative skills and cultural understandings for each unit of instruction.

Creativity and Innovation. "Creativity is about more than being able to develop an artistic product. To create or to innovate means to bring something into existence that did not exist before" (Crockett, Jukes, & Churches, 2011, p. 54). IBM (Carr, 2010) reported that creativity is considered to be the number one leadership competency of the future in a poll conducted in 2010 among 1,500 CEOs. Characteristics of creativity include curiosity, originality, imagination, and flexibility.

Creativity includes the following 21st century skills (www.p21.org):

- using a wide range of idea creation techniques such as brainstorming;
- creating new and worthwhile ideas, and then analyzing, elaborating, and refining those ideas to maximize their potential;
- developing, implementing, and communicating new ideas to others effectively;
- being open and responsive to new and diverse perspectives;
- demonstrating originality and inventiveness in work, and understanding the real-world limits to adopting new ideas; and
- viewing failure as an opportunity to learn, knowing that innovation and creativity involve risk-taking and failures before success.

In order to encourage creativity and innovation, learners need opportunities to express their thoughts and ideas, and what they have learned in a variety of ways. Gardner's theory of Multiple Intelligences (1983) values different ways to demonstrate learning and solve problems. Gardner also describes characteristics of learners according to the nine different intelligences he has identified, giving valuable examples of how to differentiate instruction to meet the needs of all learners. Multiple Intelligences Theory opens the door to creativity and innovation for both teachers and learners.

Encouraging learners to use their imagination is another way to foster creativity and innovation. When learners enter a language classroom, they walk into a different world and assume a new identity as they try to speak and act like a native speaker of the language they are learning.

Multiple Intelligences. Gardner (1983) states that intelligence is the ability to solve problems, or to create products that are valued in one or more cultural settings. Gardner believes that all human beings possess the nine intelligences he has identified, but some intelligences are stronger than others in an individual. Given the complexities of today's world, the rapidly changing needs of people throughout the world, Sir Ken Robinson (2011) states: "Now, more than ever, human communities depend on a diversity of talents; not on a singular conception of ability" (p. 109). In the language classroom, learners use a variety of skills and talents to show how they can use the target language successfully. They may write a play, story, or blog; film a day in the life of a teenager; create an infographic comparing how they and their peers from the target culture spend their time; or create a rap or song about a topic of interest.

The nine intelligences identified by Gardner (1999) are presented in Table 10 and include characteristics of the learner and learning activities that are compatible to the intelligence identified.

Table 10. Multiple Intelligences, Learner Characteristics, and Appropriate Learning Activities (Gardner, 1999)

Intelligence	Characteristics of Learner	Appropriate Learning Activities
Verbal-Linguistic	• Has a good memory for names, places, dates, and trivia • Enjoys word games • Spells words accurately • Appreciates nonsense rhymes, puns, tongue twisters, etc. • Enjoys listening to the spoken word • Has a good vocabulary for his/her age • Communicates to others in a highly verbal way	• Large- and small-group discussions, lectures, debates • Books, worksheets, manuals • Brainstorming • Writing activities • Word games • Sharing time • Storytelling, speeches, reading to class • Talking books and cassettes • Extemporaneous speaking • Journal keeping • Choral reading • Individualized reading • Memorizing linguistic facts • Recording one's words • Using word processors • Publishing (e.g., creating class newspapers)
Mathematical-Logical	• Asks a lot of questions about how things work • Computes arithmetic questions in his/her head quickly • Enjoys the challenges of math class • Finds math games and math computer games interesting • Enjoys playing chess, checkers, or other strategy games • Enjoys working with logic puzzles and brainteasers • Likes to experiment in a way that shows higher order thinking processes • Thinks on a more abstract levels than peers • Has a good sense of cause and effect relationships for his/her age	• Mathematical problems on the board • Design and conduct an experiment • Make up analogies to explain • Describe the patterns • Socratic questioning • Scientific demonstrations • Logical problem-solving exercises • Creating codes • Logic puzzles and games • Classifications and categorizations • Quantifications and calculations • Computer programming languages • Science thinking • Logical-sequential presentation of subject matter

Table 10. Multiple Intelligences, Learner Characteristics, and Appropriate Learning Activities (Gardner, 1999) (continued)

Intelligence	Characteristics of Learner	Appropriate Learning Activities
Musical	• Remembers the melody of songs • Has a good singing voice • Plays a musical instrument or sings in a choir or other musical group • Has a rhythmic way of speaking and/or moving • Unconsciously hums to him/herself • Taps rhythmically on the table or desk as he/she works • Is sensitive to the environmental noises, like rain on the roof • Can easily imitate the voices and inflections of others	• Singing, humming, whistling • Playing recorded music • Playing live music on piano, guitar, or other instruments • Group singing • Mood music • Music appreciation • Playing percussion instruments • Rhythms, songs, raps, chants • Using background music • Linking old tunes with concepts • Creating new melodies for concepts • Music software
Visual-Spatial	• Reports clear visual images • Reads maps, charts, and diagrams more easily than text • Daydreams more than peers • Enjoys art activities • Draws figures and pictures that are advanced for age • Likes to view movies, slides, or other visual presentations • Enjoys doing puzzles, mazes, "Where's Waldo?" or "hidden picture" or "I spy"- types activities • Builds interesting three-dimensional constructions for age (Legos) • Gets more out of pictures than words when reading • Doodles on workbooks, worksheets, or other materials	• Visualization • Photography • Videos, slides, and movies • Visual puzzles and mazes • 3-D construction kits • Art appreciation • Imaginative storytelling • Picture metaphors • Creative daydreaming • Painting, collage, visual arts • Visual thinking exercises • Using mind-maps and other visual organizers • Computer graphics software • Visual awareness activities • Optical illusions • Color cues • Telescopes, microscopes, and binoculars
Bodily-Kinesthetic	• Excels in one or more sports • Moves, twitches, taps, fidgets while seated for a long time in one spot • Cleverly mimics other people's gestures and mannerisms • Loves to take things apart and put them back together again • Has trouble keeping his/her hands off something new that they have just seen • Enjoys jumping, wrestling, or similar activities • Shows skill on a craft or good fine-motor coordination in other ways • Has dramatic way of expressing him/herself	• Field trips • Competitive and cooperative games • Physical awareness and relaxation exercises • All hands-on activities • Crafts • Use of kinesthetic imagery • Cooking, gardening, and other "messy" activities • Manipulatives—objects you use to learn with • Virtual reality software • Communicating with body language/hand signals • Tactile materials and experiences
Interpersonal	• Seems to be a natural leader • Gives advice to friends who have problems • Seems to be people smart—attuned to others • Belongs to clubs, committees, or other organizations • Enjoys informally teaching other kids • Likes to play games with other kids • Has two or more close friends • Has a good sense of empathy or concern for others • Others seek out his/her company	• Cooperative groups • Interpersonal interaction • Conflict mediation • Peer teaching • Board games • Cross-age tutoring • Group brainstorming sessions • Peer sharing • Community involvement • Apprenticeships • Simulations • Parties/social gatherings as context for learning

Table 10. Multiple Intelligences, Learner Characteristics, and Appropriate Learning Activities (Gardner, 1999) (continued)

Intelligence	Characteristics of Learner	Appropriate Learning Activities
Intrapersonal	• Has a realistic sense of his/her strengths and weaknesses • Does well when left alone to play or study • Marches to the beat of a different drummer in his/her style of living and learning • Has an interest or hobby that he or she doesn't talk about much • Has a good sense of self-direction • Prefers working alone to working with others • Accurately expresses how he/she is feeling • Is able to learn from his/her failures and successes • Has high self-esteem	• Set and pursue a goal • Independent study • Describe one of your personal values • Assess your own work • Self-paced instruction • Individualized projects and games • Private spaces for study • One-minute reflection periods • Interest centers • Personal connections • Options for homework • Choice time • Self-teaching programmed instruction
Naturalistic	• Has a strong affinity to the outside world, to the beauty in nature, or to animals • Enjoys subjects, shows, or stories that deal with animals or natural phenomena • May show unusual interest in subjects like biology, zoology, botany, geology, meteorology, or astronomy • Is keenly aware of his/her surroundings and changes in the environment • Has highly developed senses that help him/her notice similarities, differences, and changes in his/her surroundings • May be able to categorize or catalogue things easily • May notice things others might may not be aware of • Likes to collect, classify, or read about things from nature — rocks, fossils, butterflies, feathers, shells, and the like	• Camping • Hiking • Scuba diving • Bird watching • Gardening • Climbing • Likes sitting quietly and noticing the subtle differences
Existential	• The ability to be sensitive to, or have the capacity for, conceptualizing or tackling deeper or larger questions about human existence, such as the meaning of life, why are we born, why do we die, what is consciousness, or how did we get here • May have unique questions, insights, and perspectives about things spiritual or metaphysical • Children with a sixth sense or deep connections with earlier periods of time	• Discussion • Journaling • Reading

The learner characteristics and learning activities outlined in Table 10 provide a wealth of ideas for purposeful practice of the target language. We know that learners need multiple opportunities to use new structures, patterns, and vocabulary in order to internalize them. We also know that "drill and kill" is not an effective strategy. By varying the types of activities, learners stay engaged and are more likely to remember the new language patterns and vocabulary. Drawing on a variety of learning activities across the intelligences is one way to accommodate the needs of diverse learners. If, for example, a learner is having difficulty remembering a linguistic pattern that is practiced orally in pairwork activities (Interpersonal Intelligence), it could be helpful for the learner to physically construct the pattern using cards, each with a different word that is part of the linguistic pattern (Bodily-Kinesthetic Intelligence). Asking learners to help design different ways to practice and remember the target language using different intelligences encourages them to be creative while building their communication skills.

Imagination. In the language classroom, learners are constantly being asked to tap into their imagination to place themselves in a context or situation within the target culture in order to make the communication seem "real." Danesi (2003) identifies several meaningful contexts that engage learners' imaginations as they practice using the languages they are learning. Among them are:

- **cultural contexts** such as buying a train ticket or shopping in a market;
- **situational contexts** such as giving instructions to someone on how to prepare a certain food;
- **identification contexts** where, for example, a learner becomes a famous person from the target culture or, as in some classes, where the learners choose a new name from the target culture and take on a new identity; and
- **information-giving contexts** where learners share information they have learned about the target culture with others, such as giving advice on what to see when someone is going to travel to a country that speaks the target language.

Another context that capitalizes on imagination is the story. Egan (1986) notes that the oral tradition of storytelling is how people preserved their history and culture over time. People remembered important events, people, traditions, and ideas because these elements were woven into imaginative stories. Curtain and Dahlberg (2010) suggest that teachers design lessons according to the qualities of a good story with a clear-cut beginning, middle, and end. Other strategies that storytellers use to engage the imagination and facilitate memory include:

- **images:** encouraging learners to generate images in the mind from words engages the imagination and strengthens memory of the words;
- **rhyme and rhythm:** creating rhymes and rhythms to remember words and phrases requires imagination;
- **jokes and humor:** certain jokes can help make language visible and greatly aid awareness and control of language;
- **play:** creating imaginary worlds where learners take on new identities and roles makes learning fun, lessening the stress/anxiety learners feel when attempting something new; and
- **personalized narratives:** inviting learners to become part of a story as actors, narrators, and storytelling assistants builds interest and engagement.

A technique that capitalizes on imaginative storytelling in language classrooms is TPRS (Teaching Proficiency Through Reading and Storytelling), developed by Blaine Ray, a Spanish teacher in Bakersfield, California, in 1990. TPRS attributes its success to the fact that the focus of instruction is on the learners, providing them with lots of positive feedback and encouragement as they are acquiring a new language (www.tprstories.com). Teachers personalize stories with the goal of maintaining the interest of the learners by making them characters and active participants in the stories. As the setting of a story is developed, the reader/listener is often transported to another place and time allowing him/her to experience other ways of life and other cultures. The learners hear and practice the stories multiple times through a variety of creative repetitions in the target language.

Collaboration and Cross-Cultural Understanding. In today's globally connected world, learners can just as easily connect with peers in the same classroom as they can with peers around the world. Through the power of technology, learners can develop teamwork skills by working with peers from different cultures representing different perspectives on projects of mutual interest and importance. Collaboration and Cross-Cultural Understanding include the following 21st century skills (www.p21.org):

- working effectively and respectfully with diverse teams locally and internationally representing different social and cultural backgrounds;
- exercising flexibility and willingness to compromise to accomplish a common goal; and
- assuming shared responsibility for collaborative work, and valuing the individual contributions made by each team member.

Cooperative and Collaborative Learning. Working in small groups is a fundamental structure of language classroom activities. In the context of developing 21st century skills, we refer to cooperative learning as learners working together in groups, most often within the same classroom. We describe collaborative learning as learners connecting to people around the world via technology. Prensky (2012) advocates teaching learners to collaborate in online communities in order to be prepared for today's work world. He encourages groups of learners in one location to work on the same question or project with learners in another location, connected by technology. Both cooperative learning and collaborative learning in online communities encourage learners to take ownership for their own learning, resolve conflicts, and improve interpersonal communication skills. What is important is that diverse perspectives come together that lead to greater understanding and possible solutions to the issues being discussed.

Small groups facilitate speaking by learners for longer amounts of time and foster the sharing of ideas. They allow learners to explore essential questions from different perspectives. The teacher can monitor the quality and quantity of language used among the learners. In addition to the observations of the teacher, learners can evaluate their own participation and the participation of the group as a whole and of individuals within the group. Sample tools to evaluate group work are available at www.actfl.org/publications/books-and-brochures/the-keys-planning-learning.

Working in a small group cooperatively requires respecting these principles adapted from Johnson and Johnson (1999):

1. **Safe environment:** Learners must feel safe in sharing their ideas; there is no room for making fun of someone's ideas or dismissing them as unimportant.

2. **Clear objectives:** Learners need to know what the group is to accomplish via clear directions and clear evaluation criteria.

3. **Equal participation:** All learners are responsible for equal contribution to the work. No one can remain silent, no one can be left out.

4. **Positive interdependence:** All learners are responsible for parts of the task that are required for the successful completion of the task. No one can be assigned to a task that is non-essential to the final product produced by the group.

5. **Individual accountability:** Each learner should self-assess his or her contributions to the task, and the group should honestly assess the individual contributions of each group member and the collaboration of the group as a whole.

6. **Resolution of conflicts:** Learners have learned procedures and protocols for resolving conflicts within the group.

Collaborative and cooperative groups need real-world topics or projects to pursue in order for the group work to be successful. For example, in a collaborative online project, learners in a Spanish class in the United States might connect to a class in Argentina to discuss the importance of education for all children around the world. In preparation for the online collaboration, learners in both locations would need to research the topic, and then generate questions they would like to explore during the online collaboration. The two groups would then have to come to consensus on a final list of questions before the actual online discussion.

In a unit about healthy lifestyles, learners might work in cooperative groups to dramatize an ideal daily routine. Each group would have to come to consensus on what to include in the daily routine, how they are going to represent it, and what role each group member will play. To facilitate equal participation of all group members during the planning phase, the teacher could give each person a scoring guide to track their contributions to the group (Table 11).

Table 11. Scoring Guide for Cooperative Learning Group Project

	Yes	No
I suggested ideas for the storyline for the video.		
I added to other group members' suggestions for the storyline.		
I listened respectfully to other group members.		
Each member of the group has a speaking role in the story.		
Our group equally shared responsibilities for creating the storyline for the video.		
Our group cooperated to complete the outline for the story by the end of class.		

Interculturality. The concept of interculturality is a mindset, a way of being with the global community. It begins in the classroom as learners work in pairs and small groups, listening to other people's ideas with an open mind, being willing to work cooperatively with others. Collaborating with classrooms around the world to explore a mutual topic of interest gives learners the opportunity to hear opinions and perspectives that may be different from theirs.

Learners can establish baseline data on where they are in terms of interculturality using statements such as these:

- I know that several languages are spoken in my country.
- I know which languages are spoken in my country.
- I can list several languages that are spoken in my country.
- I can recognize several languages when I hear them spoken.
- I can recognize the written form of several languages.
- I know people who live in another country.
- I know that people living in the United States have different cultural backgrounds.
- I like tasting dishes from different countries.
- I know and/or can sing songs from another country.
- I can give an example of a festival celebrated in another region/country.

- I can name several examples of regional dishes from the United States.
- I can name several examples of dishes from other countries.
- I have visited museums or seen films presenting the cultures of different countries.
- I know characters from stories, animated films, and cartoons from other countries. (www.coe.int/t/dg4/education/elp/elp-reg/Source/Templates/ELP_Language_Biography_Intercultural_Component_Templates_EN.doc)

Learners can document their growth in terms of interculturality through reflection and journaling. The European Language Portfolio project (Little & Simpson, 2003) recommends that learners reflect on intercultural experiences using these four questions as guides:

1. Where, with whom, and in what context did the experience take place?
2. What kind of experience was it in terms of intensity?
3. What was my response? Did I merely reflect on the experience, or did it prompt me to some kind of action?
4. Why did I respond in the way I did?

Increasing their awareness of all the ways their lives connect to other cultures, and reflecting on their interactions with people from other cultures, is the first step in developing skills of interculturality among learners.

> The Department of Public Instruction of North Carolina in cooperation with the National Council of State Supervisors for Languages (NCSSFL) created a video series on the implementation and use of LinguaFolio, including a discussion of interculturality. It is located at: www.learnnc.org/lp/editions/linguafolio/6122.
>
> The Center for Applied Second Language Studies (CASLS) at the University of Oregon offers an electronic version of LinguaFolio. It is located at: https://linguafolio.uoregon.edu/.

The Instructional Repertoire, organized around the 4 Cs—Communication, Critical Thinking and Problem Solving, Creativity and Innovation, Collaboration and Cross-Cultural Understanding—of the 21st Century Skills, gives language teachers a variety of tools designed to engage all learners purposefully in building their communication skills and cultural understandings. Earlier in the chapter, the Standards for Learning Languages and the ACTFL Proficiency Guidelines were introduced as the foundation for curriculum design, and included a visual reminding us that effective curriculum design relates to the learner on a personal level (*Knowing Myself*), to where the learner lives locally, regionally, nationally (*Exploring Communities*), and globally (*Engaging with the World*). The next chapter will consider thematic unit design in more detail and will present a template for designing a standards-based thematic unit.

Application

1. Your department has been asked to write a paragraph for the school newsletter explaining how languages are addressing the hyper-connected learner of the 21st century. What will you write?
2. You've been asked to define interculturality. What would you say? What examples would you share?

Reflection

1. How am I promoting the development of cultural awareness in my classroom? Are there specific ways that I might address this awareness more explicitly?
2. Do learners benefit from having an understanding of terms like proficiency and interculturality? Why or why not? How do I build awareness of these concepts in my classrooms?

Chapter 2 | Unit Design

To begin with the end in mind means to start with a clear understanding of your destination. It means to know where you are going so that you better understand where you are now so that the steps you take are always in the right direction.

— *Stephen Covey*

Why Is a Standards-Based and Text-Rich Approach to Unit Design Recommended?

Learners acquire language best in meaningful contexts. Authentic texts, those that are created by speakers of the language for speakers of the language, provide an ideal starting point for a thematic unit by establishing a meaningful context. Authentic written, spoken, or visual texts also guarantee that language is not separated from culture since authentic text embeds culture in the text itself. Mickan (2013) explains how even something as simple as a poster offering a reward for a lost dog tells us something about the culture of a people. That poster allows the reader to know that the culture values dogs, that dogs are part of the family, and that the relationship between an owner and pet is important as indicated by the offer of a reward. The language used in the poster is meaningful because it is embedded in a context that communicates a message. As learners develop a linguistic and cultural understanding of the text, they are more likely to want to discuss the text—creating optimum conditions for meaningful communication to occur. More importantly, learners are likely to retain what they are learning because what is being learned is contextualized and has meaning.

Why Are Themes Important in Unit Design?

Think back to when you were a child or think about a child with whom you interact often today. You probably can recall a point in time where you or that child became curious about something. Interest in a topic may have been the result of something seen on TV, a gift or toy, or possibly an experience like a trip to the zoo. Suddenly, you were doing all that you could to learn more about that topic, consulting a variety of resources—reading, watching documentaries, talking to others, and visiting appropriate sites. Your knowledge of the topic increased, your vocabulary associated with the topic became increasingly more precise and you found yourself asking more questions about the topic. The complexity of the text was not the determining factor; you were simply interacting with the text because of inherent interest or curiosity. Your interest may have continued or it may have waned before moving on to other topics of interest. The conditions for motivation were met—mastery, autonomy, and purpose. You were attempting to learn all that you could about the topic, you had selected a topic of interest and you knew why you were investigating the topic (Pink, 2009).

A thematic unit attempts to recreate this natural curiosity by allowing for exploration of a topic in greater depth. Thematic units allow for the development of topics that are organized around goals based on the Standards for Learning Languages and other relevant standards. Teachers gain increased control over the curriculum as they select topics that are likely to be of interest to their learners and materials that will introduce the topic in ways that invite learner inquiry. By design, thematic units incorporate a "less is more" approach allowing learners to focus on a topic in some depth. Thematic units have the potential to alleviate some of the more commonly heard complaints about the general lack of time for in-depth study given the number of chapters required in a curriculum based on a textbook. Learners need time to process new information if they are to truly learn. They need time to connect new learning to prior knowledge and experiences and they need adequate time to process new information through multiple, interactive experiences. They require an environment that addresses the brain's curiosity and need for novelty (Caine & Caine, 1990).

How many summers have teachers spent writing or rewriting curriculum when new textbooks or new materials were adopted? Thematic units are created independent of textbooks and other similar materials, so the emphasis is on revision and not rewriting the entire curriculum. It can be disconcerting to lose the security of the predetermined scope and sequence of a textbook, and teachers may worry that learners need that type of structure. Yet research indicates that the use of thematic units is valuable for a number of reasons. Hale and Cunningham (2011) analyzed how first graders who had low literacy skills in English performed during a 10-week thematic unit called "All People Need Shelter." First graders read and wrote about a variety of shelters—igloos, *tipis*, castles, log cabins, and adobes. The group participating in the thematic unit showed statistically significant improvement through quantitative measures of vocabulary, reading level, and written expression. Teachers' and learners' comments were also positive with regard to motivation.

Thematic units such as this one on shelter allow for multiple entry points as learners engage in the topic. As teachers identify materials for the unit, they begin to pull together a collection of materials from different genres, media, and reading levels. Individual learners who have different interests and varying proficiency levels benefit from being able to learn about the topic using a variety of materials. These materials or text sets allow teachers to accommodate learners at their level, while still allowing each individual learner equal access to the topic. Additionally, learners benefit by reading about a topic in different genres, and the variety of texts also allows learners to consider different points of view on the topic (Lent, 2012). Thematic units also allow learners to explore both literary and informational texts, thus addressing one of the Common Core key considerations calling for learners to be able to read and comprehend a variety of complex literary and informational text independently and proficiently (www.corestandards.org).

"Less is More." The "less is more" aphorism is one of the nine principles of the Coalition of Essential Schools. It requires that learners be given the chance to develop solid understanding of concepts rather than simply taking time to explore numerous topics in a superficial way. The "less is more" principle reflects

that learners need time to work with what they are learning in meaningful ways in order to retain it. (Cushman, 1994)

Research in vocabulary acquisition also supports the concept of "less is more." Vocabulary is key to learning a language and the expanded amount of time on a topic allows for acquisition of new vocabulary by allowing learners time to acquire vocabulary in context before being required to use it in increasingly more involved tasks. Learning a new word is not just a factor of how many times a learner encounters a word (incidental learning), but is more a factor of how often the learner is able to use the new word in a meaningful context (intentional learning). Barcroft's (2004) fifth principle of effective vocabulary instruction states that there is a need to progress from less demanding to more demanding vocabulary-related activities. Clearly, teachers need time to create the contexts where learners can use and recycle vocabulary in meaningful ways (Barcroft, 2004; Selivan, 2010).

What Is the Mindset for Thematic Unit Design?

A well-designed unit is the foundation for planning and delivering instruction. Based on the Standards for Learning Languages and the considerable library of research related to effective instruction, we suggest that units be designed around five basic principles. These principles are expansions of Helena Curtain's three requirements that units be cognitively engaging, intrinsically interesting, and culturally connected (personal communication, 2012). The units should be:

- Communicatively purposeful: Building toward proficiency
- Culturally focused: Developing interculturality
- Intrinsically interesting: Relevant to learners
- Cognitively engaging: Requiring critical thinking skills
- Standards-based: Reflecting goals for learning languages

Consider the education unit that was outlined in Chapter 1. The essential question, "Why can't all children go to school?" allows the learner to consider the topic from the perspective of self, the community, and the world. The theme is culturally focused, providing the opportunity to explore attitudes towards school and issues related to school attendance locally, nationally, and internationally. The essential question is framed as a global issue, allowing learners to apply what they are learning to address the problem of schooling in a creative way and the performance tasks for the unit provide opportunities and purpose for meaningful communication. Finally, the unit is standards-based, incorporating each of the goal areas for learning languages. Table 12 summarizes how the principles of the mindset for unit design are present in the unit on education.

Table 12. Mindset for Development of Thematic Unit on Education

Mindset	Sample Connections to the Unit
Communicatively Purposeful	• Essential question and unit goals ask learners to explore why all children can't go to school
Culturally Focused	• Extensive use of authentic texts • Focus on school attendance, required/optional classes (products, practices, perspectives)
Intrinsically Interesting	• Choice in how information is shared with others • Theme has a strong personal connection and links to the community and world (interculturality)
Cognitively Engaging	• Research reasons why all children cannot go to school • Evaluate global efforts to address school attendance
Standards-Based	• Communication–explore why all children cannot go to school • Cultures–focus on education around the world • Connections–connect to Social Studies: educational systems • Comparisons–examine importance of school • Communities–collaborate with another school

What Are Global Themes for Learning Languages?

Thematic units shift instructional focus from language for the sake of language to the use of language to achieve meaningful goals. The theme creates a meaningful context allowing teachers to select texts that engage the learner in more complex thinking, allowing for a more sophisticated use of the language. Thematic units also offer a more natural setting for narrative structure and task-based organization of content (Curtain & Dahlberg, 2010). By working with themes in real-world contexts, learners are able to consider how the content of the thematic unit connects to their lives, their communities, and to the world. They use their communicative skills in the three modes to access and discuss new information and to share their learning with others. Figure 6 reintroduces the visual of the curriculum framework as a reminder of how communication skills and interculturality develop through the 5 Cs, and adds the global themes as the context for language learning in the 21st century.

Figure 6. Curriculum Design for Learning Languages in the 21st Century with Global Themes

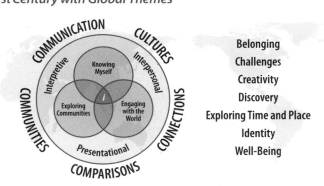

Belonging
Challenges
Creativity
Discovery
Exploring Time and Place
Identity
Well-Being

Multi-dimensional themes allow learners to consider topics from a multicultural perspective, as the learners look first in the mirror to explore self and their immediate home environment, and then look out the window of the home to view other communities and the world. Learners use the mirror to reflect on their own experiences and the window as they consider the perspectives of others. Themes invite learners to make connections and consider topics from different perspectives. The themes—Belonging, Challenges, Creativity, Discovery, Exploring Time and Place, Identity, and Well-Being—can be tailored for use in all language learning program models and used to guide unit design in the 21st century. These themes invite teachers and learners to build communication and interculturality by exploring a variety of topics through the lenses of self, community, and the world.

Let's consider how these global themes apply to the unit on education presented in Chapter 1. The topic of education could be connected to several of the individual themes. For example, education could be connected to Well-Being since a person's level of education can impact the quality of life. The unit could be part of Exploring Time and Place if the intent is to focus primarily on school as an institution in the past, present, and future and its impact on society. Creativity or Discovery might be the theme if learners are asked to consider their school as a place that fosters both creativity and discovery, making comparisons to other educational systems and offering suggestions for innovation based on what they learn. A class that wanted to focus on teenagers and the influence of peer groups might select Belonging or Identity as the theme. Perhaps the most important consideration is how relevant a unit theme and topic are to a particular group of learners. The curriculum mindset introduced earlier suggests that selection of a theme and topic be evaluated by asking the following questions:

- What is the cultural focus that allows for ongoing reflection on interculturality?
- How will learners communicate in purposeful ways?
- Why is this unit of study of interest to learners?
- How will they apply or transfer their learning to new situations?
- How does this unit address the Standards and other standards required by my school?

In the unit on education, the essential question, "Why can't all children go to school?" presents an issue of global importance. Therefore, the theme of Challenges begins to frame the learning for the unit. Let's consider the role of essential questions in relation to the global themes.

Essential Questions. McTighe and Wiggins (2013) offer three connotations for the word "essential" and state that all three are valid in defining essential questions. The first type of essential question refers to a question that is important and timeless. These questions are broad in scope and can be discussed without ever arriving at a single answer. As understanding deepens, answers may change and become increasingly more nuanced. These questions promote learner inquiry and thinking and cause learners to learn how to learn. The second type of question is considered to be "elemental" or "foundational" to a discipline. These questions surface frequently among experts and are often the subject of debate and research within a field of study. The final category of essential questions allows for questions that are vital or necessary for understanding core content—the facts or skills that learners must learn in order to be able to transfer or apply the knowledge and skills that they are learning. Table 13 provides examples of each type of essential question in the context of language learning.

Table 13. Types of Essential Questions in the Context of Language Learning

Essential Questions		
Important and Timeless *(broad, no single answer)*	**Elemental or Foundational** *(debated by experts in the discipline)*	**Content-Related** *(specific to discipline)*
What is art? What is the relationship between man and nature? What is wellness?	What is interculturality and how is it assessed? What does it mean to be fluent in a language?	What awareness and understandings of products, practices, and perspectives are needed to enter into another culture? What literacy skills do I need to succeed as a global citizen?

A thematic unit is normally organized around an essential question that serves to focus both teaching and learning. Essential questions benefit learners by inviting inquiry. They identify at the start of the unit what learners are going to explore, helping them focus on the knowledge and skills that they need in order to begin to formulate answers that address the unit question. Essential questions allow for differentiation by asking all learners to consider the same question even though the process for considering the question may vary according to individual needs.

Consider the question, "What is art?" in Table 13. Keeping in mind that this question does not have a specific answer, let's examine how a young child in kindergarten and a novice learner in middle school might answer the question. The kindergartner might respond with thumbs up or thumbs down when shown an image to indicate if the image represents art or not. The teacher might model, "What is art?" and then point to different examples saying, "This is art" or "This is not art." The child might then be able to point and say, "This is art." The novice middle school learner might be able to answer in a more abstract manner saying, "Art is controversial, original, personal, beautiful, timeless." This type of response can only occur if the teacher predetermines and introduces key vocabulary through a variety of learning activities including authentic texts.

Essential questions benefit teachers by helping to clarify and prioritize content that is truly important. Often teachers believe that everything they are supposed to teach is of equal importance and connected because it is all related to learning the language. An essential question focuses the unit and makes it easier to let go of content that has traditionally been taught, but is no longer relevant.

Essential questions are not easy to write. It makes sense to craft an essential question as you begin to develop the unit, but essential questions are truly a genre of writing and they will be improved by going through drafting, revising, and editing as the unit is developed (McTighe & Wiggins, 2013). Keep in mind that an effective essential question is open-ended, invites inquiry, and, for the language classroom, is one that learners can begin to answer in the target language. This does not mean that essential questions need to be limited to what a learner can explicitly answer, but rather that the teacher must think carefully about how to help learners use the language that they already know in combination with what they are learning. The Novice High or Intermediate Low learner might answer the question, "Why can't all children go to school?" by saying, "Some children don't go to school because of war in their country." As learners become familiar with the concept of essential questions, they can assist in the development of questions for a unit of study. We have created sample essential questions for each of the global themes at the Novice, Intermediate, and Advanced levels (see Appendix G).

Additional Resources for Thematic Instruction. ACTFL, Advanced Placement (AP) from The College Board, and the International Baccalaureate (IB) offer additional resources for thematic teaching and learning. Learning scenarios for several different languages can be found in the *Standards for Foreign Language Learning in the 21st Century Revised 3rd Edition* (NSFLEP, 2006). These learning scenarios explain the context of a thematic unit and then name the Standards that are addressed in those units. Titles such as Buildings Tell a Story, Market Day, Moroccan Showcase, All in the Family, Immigration and Heritage, Photographs Have a Voice, Let's Stay Healthy, Birds Beyond Borders, The Legend of Corn, and Stereotypes and Prejudice suggest themes and topics that incorporate language, culture, and content.

The curricula for both AP and IB language courses advocate a thematic approach to language learning by naming themes and suggesting contexts or topics that allow learners to explore each theme. Both use themes as the frameworks for their exams and we encourage teachers in language programs connected to AP or IB to use those themes in their classrooms. Learners in those programs need to be familiar with and work frequently in the context of those themes. Table 14 names the themes that are required by AP and those that are required and optional for the IB.

Table 14. Advanced Placement (AP) and International Baccalaureate (IB) Themes

Advanced Placement (AP) Themes	International Baccalaureate (IB) Themes
Global Challenges	Communication and Media
Personal and Public Identities	Global Issues
Contemporary Life	Social Relationships
Science and Technology	Cultural Diversity
Beauty and Aesthetics	Customs and Traditions
Families and Communities	Leisure
	Health
	Science and Technology

What Are the Steps in Designing a Thematic Unit?

Let's begin the process of creating a standards-based thematic unit. The remainder of this chapter will walk you through the completion of a unit template using the unit A Balanced Lifestyle as a model. Before reading the rest of this chapter, you may find it helpful to review the completed unit for A Balanced Lifestyle (see Appendix H). You may also wish to print a copy of the blank template (see Appendix I). Both templates are also available online at www.actfl.org/publications/books-and-brochures/the-keys-planning-learning. Although it may be tempting to read quickly through the information that is presented here, we believe that it will be more beneficial to read a section, review the example, and then pause to consider a unit that you would like to develop.

Language and Level, Theme and Topic, Essential Question. The initial fields of the template ask for the language and level of the unit, the theme and topic, and the essential question that will frame the unit. Table 15 shows the first section of the unit template.

Table 15. Unit Template: Language and Level, Theme and Topic, Essential Question

Language and Level/Grade	French – Novice Mid➔Novice High
Theme/Topic	**Well-Being:** A Balanced Lifestyle
Essential Question	How do people here and in (the French-speaking world) describe a balanced lifestyle?

This thematic unit plan is designed for learners in the Novice range (Novice Mid to Novice High) who might be in a course that is often called French 1, Japanese 1, or Latin 1, for example. The proficiency range is often more indicative of the level of language in the classroom given the wide variety of program models that exist. Additional information on proficiency levels is located in Appendix B. While the example outlined here is specific to French language classes, it is a unit topic that transfers easily to other languages and one that could be adjusted for higher proficiency levels. It is also a theme that elementary, middle, and high school learners can explore and one that captures elements of topics that are often found in textbooks. The global theme Well-Being frames the unit. The essential question is open-ended and is likely to be revisited by individuals at different stages of their lives. From a language perspective, it is also a question that Novice learners can answer in the target language.

Unit Goals. Begin by determining the relevant goals for the unit. The most effective curriculum is written in terms of what learners can do. Table 16 shows the goals for the unit.

Table 16. Unit Template: Goals

Goals *What should learners know and be able to do by the end of the unit?*	Learners will be able to: • Explore health and wellness websites to identify elements of a balanced lifestyle here and in (country in the French-speaking world). • Compare lifestyles of teenagers to teenagers in (country in the French-speaking world) in terms of balance. • Make recommendations for ways to create or maintain a balanced lifestyle. • Create a presentation for (the community) highlighting ways to promote a balanced lifestyle.

The goals that are written here indicate the performance targets that will guide the unit (Wiggins & McTighe, 1998). The goals address the Standards for Learning Languages and incorporate the three modes by creating a context and purpose for communication. The unit goals indicate what a successful learner will know and be able to do. They are written in ways that make the unit relevant to the learners' lives and describe tasks that might occur in the real world. These goals do not indicate the vocabulary and structures that need to be learned. Those are considered later after the summative performance assessment tasks have been determined.

Consider the following questions as you review the unit goals created for the unit A Balanced Lifestyle:

• Are the goals relevant in today's world? Do they have the potential to engage the learner?
• Do learners acquire new knowledge and skills beyond (French) language, and culture?
• Do the goals convey a purpose for communication in each mode?
• Do the goals integrate culture, language, and content?
• Do the goals provide an opportunity to use language beyond the classroom?

It's clear that the unit focuses on comparing lifestyles in different communities allowing for the integration of the Cultures and Comparisons goals. The learners acquire information about health and wellness as part of a balanced lifestyle and are likely to address the Connections goal as they explore that topic. Finally, learners will present some of what they have learned beyond the classroom, allowing them to address the Communities goal area. Although the specifics of how each standard will be addressed are not yet identified, the unit goals do integrate the 5 Cs of the Standards.

> ✓ **Pause to consider your unit.** Who are the learners? What theme and topic will you address? What is the "working" essential question? What are the unit goals?

Summative Performance Assessment. The summative performance assessment tasks are presented next to reflect Understanding by Design (1998), beginning with the end in mind. Learners must know at the beginning of the unit how they will demonstrate learning by the end of the unit, and they must know how their work will be assessed. Knowing where they are headed in terms of performance allows learners to focus their attention in ways that guide their efforts to meet the performance goals of the unit. Just as the thematic unit is organized around goals based on the Standards for Learning Languages and other relevant standards, so too are the summative assessment tasks. The template allows for multiple assessments in the interpretive mode in support of the Common Core English Language Arts (ELA) Anchor standards for reading, requiring that learners integrate and evaluate information from multiple sources, and compare how different texts address the same theme (www.corestandards.org). Table 17 shows the summative performance assessment tasks for the unit.

Table 17. Unit Template: Summative Performance Assessment Tasks

Summative Performance Assessment	Interpretive Mode		
• *These tasks allow learners to demonstrate how well they have met the goals of the unit.* • *They are integrated throughout the unit.* • *The template encourages multiple interpretive tasks.* • *The interpretive tasks inform the content of the presentational and interpersonal tasks.* • *The tasks should incorporate 21st century skills.*	Learners will read a blog written by a teenager where he discusses his activities. They will demonstrate comprehension by answering questions about main ideas and will complete a graphic organizer based on information found in the text.	Learners will watch a commercial for a product that promises to make life easier or less stressful and will demonstrate comprehension by analyzing the effectiveness of the message and product.	Learners will read a schedule of a top athlete to determine how he spends the hours in his day deciding what elements are part of a balanced lifestyle and what is missing.
	Presentational Mode		Interpersonal Mode
	Learners will create a presentation based on multiple sources of information highlighting ways to promote a balanced lifestyle for teenagers. The presentation will be shared with another French class.		In pairs or small groups, learners share what they have learned about their lifestyle and the lifestyle of teenagers in (France) in terms of a balanced lifestyle. They compare their daily routines and schedules and make and respond to suggestions to adjust their lifestyle.

The summative performance tasks also address the 4 Cs of the 21st Century Skills. *Communication* is assessed in each mode. Learners *collaborate* in the interpersonal mode to discuss balance in their lifestyles. In the presentational mode, they use their *creativity* to design the necessary materials to promote a more balanced lifestyle. The tasks in all three modes ask learners to *think critically and solve problems* as they analyze authentic texts in the interpretive mode, evaluate lifestyles in terms of balance during group discussions, and seek solutions to a wellness issue in their community. The performance tasks are not intended to take place on the last day of the unit. Instead, they are integrated throughout the unit and happen when the teacher determines that the learners are ready to demonstrate what they know and are able to do. Ways of assessing these tasks will be discussed in Chapter 4.

The Interpretive Tasks. As stated earlier, the unit template allows for multiple interpretive tasks. There are several reasons for increased focus on the interpretive mode. Mickan (2013) explains the importance of text, defining it as any communication spoken, written, or visual involving language. Mickan states:

> Texts comprise meaning potential. At the very heart of our language experience is the need to create our own meanings in response to texts. Texts set up opportunities for communication about content—for consent, for exploration of ideas, and for contestation. Each interaction with texts involves processing the meanings of what is going on at a particular moment. We appraise and assess what we read, what we write, what we hear and say. In so doing, we declare, develop, and define personal interpretations. Text encounters are opportunities for action—for expression of points of view, for argument, for dispute—and for negotiation, agreement, affirmation, and confirmation. Texts are ideal for direct engagement of learners in discussions, as they constitute discourse resources for formulation of individual and group ideas. (p. 39)

The interpretive tasks for the unit A Balanced Lifestyle convey that learners will be expected to read, listen to, and/or view a variety of texts. They will read a blog on activities, watch a commercial based on quality of life, and read the schedule of a top athlete. The interpretive tasks are shown in Table 17.

The Presentational Task. The presentational task is a spoken and/or written task that allows learners to showcase what they have learned by creating a new product that they will share with others beyond the classroom. They have time to draft, revise, and edit the presentation. Presentational tasks offer opportunities for learners to collaborate with peers in the classroom and with others in communities beyond the classroom using available technology tools. These tasks offer learners the opportunity to solve problems and to provide evidence of their ability to take what they have learned and create a new product. Quality presentational tasks move beyond written and spoken tasks that simply require learners to reproduce what they did during the unit. The audience for the performance moves beyond just the teacher and the learners in the class. The presentational task for this unit addresses the major unit goals and allows learners to begin to develop their answers to the essential question that frames the unit. Learners create a wellness promotional piece that can be shared with others either locally or globally using web-based tools. The presentational task is shown in Table 17.

The Interpersonal Task. The interpersonal task asks learners to engage with others in communication that is unrehearsed, and that calls for active negotiation of meaning. Learners engage in oral or written communication to exchange information. To build the interpersonal skill, teachers create opportunities for learners to work with the content from the unit in ways that mimic real-world conversations. The interpersonal task for this unit gives learners the opportunity to reflect on their own life and to discuss the balance in their lives as they consider what they learn from their peers and what they have learned about teenagers in other parts of the world. The interpersonal task is shown in Table 17.

> ✅ **Pause to consider your unit.** What authentic materials do you intend to use? You may want to search for authentic texts that will anchor the unit before going much further. What will your performance assessment tasks be for each mode? Revisit these tasks as you refine and further develop your unit.

Cultures. Next, teachers need to identify cultural products, practices, and perspectives within the context of the unit. The template allows for two examples, although units will include several more. Keep in mind that culture is a natural component of authentic texts—thus authentic texts selected for a unit provide rich resources for exploring the products, practices, and perspectives of another culture. Table 18 shows how the cultural components would be identified in the unit template.

Table 18. Unit Template: Cultural Products, Practices, and Perspectives

Cultures (Sample Evidence) *Indicate the relationship between the product, practice, and perspective.*	**Product:** Café **Practice:** Stopping with friends for coffee **Perspective:** It's not the coffee, it's the conversation. **Product:** School year calendar **Practice:** Regular breaks, holidays **Perspective:** Balance

The two samples from the unit A Balanced Lifestyle capture aspects of culture that are relevant to the unit theme and address specific unit goals. The concept of having a coffee with friends at a local café allows learners to consider the role the café plays in other cultures. Learners might view a clip from a movie, commenting on what they observe in a café scene—who is there, what they are doing, the position of tables and chairs,

etc. They might consider the time of day; the length of time the person is there, whether they are alone or with friends. Learners might then compare that experience to one in their own life, noting similarities and differences. Learners might work together to identify a place in their community that is similar to the café. The second example deals with school year calendars. Learners consider the cycle for vacations in the schools, making comparisons to the school calendar in their community. As learners compare schedules, they consider why different calendars exist and what those calendars say about lifestyles. They might then work together to create the ideal school year calendar for their community, taking into consideration the limitations and benefits of such a calendar.

> ✅ **Pause to consider your unit.** Consider how the authentic texts you have selected embed cultural information. What products, practices, and perspectives will you highlight in your unit?

Connections. The Connections goal area highlights the importance of learners using the target language to learn content from other disciplines while considering the perspectives that other cultures bring to that content. Learners are not just learning language; they are using their language skills to learn about a variety of topics. Table 19 shows how the content of the unit addresses the Connections goal area.

Table 19. Unit Template: Connections

Connections (Sample Evidence)	**Making Connections**	**Acquiring Information and Diverse Perspectives**
	Health and wellness: Compare recommendations for healthy lifestyles. **Media studies:** Consider impact of media on lifestyle considerations like diet and exercise.	• Differences in school schedules • Importance of vacation and family time • Tradition of *"Fermature annuelle"* (annual closing) in France

The essential question for the unit guides the learning that will take place in the classroom. Remember the essential question for this unit: "How do people here and in (the French-speaking world) describe a balanced lifestyle?" In this unit, learners connect to the content of other disciplines as they learn more about healthy lifestyles and look at the ways that media in different cultures influences consumers. Learners are encouraged to independently explore related topics of personal interest. They might read information on the importance of sleep and compare the amount of sleep they typically get with their peers in other cultures. They might then propose solutions that address the need for more sleep. Learners will consider different attitudes toward work and leisure, discussing the fact that Paris is often considered empty in August with so many people on vacation for the entire month. They might interview their parents to learn more about their vacation schedules at work and why a month-long vacation may or may not be possible.

> ✓ **Pause to consider your unit.** What other disciplines are connected to your unit theme and topic? Are learners studying aspects of the topic in other classes? Are there aspects of the topic that are perceived differently depending on where someone lives?

Comparisons. The Comparisons goal area allows learners to develop a greater understanding of their own language and culture while learning about others. It promotes reflection at the beginning of language instruction allowing learners to develop skills needed to compare and contrast elements of language and culture without making judgments. As one exchange student said frequently at the beginning of a home stay when asked what she thought about something: "It's neither bad nor good, just different." Table 20 indicates the types of comparisons that could be made in the unit.

Table 20. Unit Template: Comparisons

Comparisons (Sample Evidence)	Language Comparisons	Cultural Comparisons
	la joie de vivre (joy of living) *métro, boulot, dodo* (subway, work, sleep) *Ne t'en fais pas!* (Don't worry!) *La détente* (relaxation) Making polite recommendations	Work time/leisure time Meal time with/without family Weekend activities Walking/driving Teenagers working during school year/summer Life expectancies

Comparison of language is more than the comparison of linguistic structures; language comparisons allow learners to consider how words convey meaning. In the sample unit, learners consider language expressions that are unique to the target culture and not easily translated into another language, and determine how or if that information is conveyed in their culture. They might look at store hours or signs stating "Annual Closing" and compare that information to the advantages and disadvantages of what occurs locally. Comparison of culture

allows learners to make comparisons to their own cultures and to other cultures where the language is spoken. In today's diverse classrooms, it may also be an opportunity to bring in the cultural background of learners from other cultures. The suggested topics for this sample unit deal with elements that are part of learners' lives, but learners may also identify other cultural elements that they wish to explore. Learners might design a survey using a web-based survey tool asking teenagers in another country to share facts and personal information about the structure of a typical teenage day. That same survey might be administered to learners of the target language in a nearby community allowing for analysis of the results across cultures.

> ✓ **Pause to consider your unit.** What resources do you have that will allow you to make comparisons based on evidence in texts? What words and expressions are native speakers likely to attach to this topic?

Communities. The Communities goal area promotes involvement with both the target language and target culture communities. It is also the goal area that envisions how learners will use their skills beyond the classroom and for the rest of their lives. Access to technology has made it much easier to achieve this goal, allowing learners to reach beyond the walls of the classroom using technologies like Skype to discuss particular issues when working in the interpersonal mode, reading blogs of native speakers when working in the interpretive mode, and by having learners post their work to a wiki or blog when working in the presentational mode. Table 21 indicates how learners will apply and share their learning with others.

Table 21. Unit Template: Communities

Communities (Sample Evidence)	School and Global Communities	Lifelong Learning
	Share information on wellness with community.	Examine personal lifestyle and make adjustments as needed.

The sample unit asks learners to examine a community-based problem and offer solutions. The research may be done by interviewing learners in the target culture and/or by inviting guest speakers from a local target language community. Learners may participate in a community fair or may share their findings and solutions online or by writing a letter to the editor of a target language paper or online journal. Learners can be challenged to demonstrate their personal growth and learning by keeping a reflective journal where they comment on what they are learning, and the cultural and linguistic insights that they are acquiring as they interact with others in the target language. They may also be encouraged to set a personal learning goal or wellness goal based on what they have learned in the unit.

> ✅ **Pause to consider your unit.** How will learners extend their learning beyond their classrooms? How will what they have learned impact their lives?

English Language Arts (ELA) Common Core State Standards. As outlined earlier, there are strong connections between the ELA Common Core State Standards and the expectations found in the Standards for Learning Languages. A learner who is college and career ready demonstrates that readiness by what they are able to do. The same is true of language learners who demonstrate what they are able to do as they engage in the summative performance assessment tasks for the unit. Table 22 shows the Common Core State Standards that are emphasized in the sample unit.

The types of performance required by the summative tasks can be easily aligned to the ELA Common Core Anchor Standards for Reading, Writing, Speaking and Listening, and Language. Consider the performance tasks for the sample unit. The selected Common Core State Standards capture how learners will advance their literacy skills as they complete the required performance tasks. Interpretive tasks align with the Anchor Standards for Reading. Presentational tasks align with the Anchor Standards for Writing. Interpersonal tasks are reflected in the Anchor

Standards for Speaking and Listening. Language Standards are similar to the Proficiency Guidelines showing how learners develop accuracy and vocabulary skills over time. The Common Core Anchor Standards are listed for reference in Appendix J. Alignment with the performance assessment tasks in the three modes is included here for explanation purposes. The actual template asks just for the Common Core State Standards since the performances tasks already appear in an earlier section.

> *Aligning the National Standards for Learning Languages with the Common Core Standards* can be found at: www.actfl.org/sites/default/files/pdfs/Aligning_CCSS_Language_Standards_v6.pdf.

> ✅ **Pause to consider your unit.** Use this as an opportunity to make certain that your performance assessment tasks ask learners to perform at the higher levels of Bloom's Taxonomy. Check for evidence of 21st Century Skills—Collaboration, Critical Thinking, and Creativity. Then, consider the Common Core Anchor Standards and select those that align most closely with your assessments.

Toolbox. Now that the unit goals and assessments are in place, select the appropriate grammatical structures and vocabulary that are needed for learners to meet the unit goals. Table 23 shows the components of the Toolbox and gives a brief overview indicating the role that each element plays in the design of the unit.

Table 22. Unit Template: Common Core

Interpretive	**Reading: 1.** Read closely to determine what the text says explicitly and to make logical inferences from it; cite specific textual evidence when writing or speaking to support conclusions drawn from the text. **Language: 4.** Determine or clarify the meaning of unknown and multiple-meaning words and phrases by using context clues, analyzing meaningful word parts, and consulting general and specialized reference materials as appropriate. • *Learners will read a blog written by a teenager where he discusses his activities.* • *Learners will watch a commercial for a product that promises to make life "easier" or less stressful.* • *Learners will read a schedule of a top athlete to determine how he spends the hours in his day, deciding what elements are part of a balanced lifestyle and what is missing.*
Presentational	**Writing: 6.** Use technology, including the Internet, to produce and publish writing and to interact and collaborate with others. **Writing: 7.** Conduct short as well as more sustained research projects based on focused questions, demonstrating understanding of the subject under investigation. • *Learners will create a presentation based on multiple sources of information, highlighting ways to promote a balanced lifestyle for teenagers. The presentation will be shared with another French class.*
Interpersonal	**Speaking and Listening: 1.** Prepare for and participate effectively in a range of conversations and collaborations. • *Learners share what they have learned about their lifestyle and the lifestyle of teenagers in (France) in terms of a balanced lifestyle. They compare their daily routines and schedules and make and respond to suggestions to adjust their lifestyle.*

Let's consider each component and how it is integrated in the sample unit plan.

Language Functions. Language functions describe how we use language in our daily lives. They convey the purpose for speaking or writing by identifying the basic task that a person must be able to do in order to communicate effectively in a given situation. A list of possible functions has been created to make it easier to identify appropriate functions for addressing unit goals (see Appendix K). Table 24 provides a list of functional language statements for the sample unit.

The functions that are listed here are not broken out by mode since there is an assumption that most functions will be addressed in all modes to a greater or lesser extent. The learning activity section of this template provides further information on how language functions will be addressed in each mode. Consider the unit goals and performance assessment tasks to determine the functions that learners need in order to understand and communicate successfully in this unit. The bolded statement **Compare** is the function and the italicized *lifestyle routines* shows how the function applies to this specific unit.

> **Pause to consider your unit.** What language functions are needed to allow learners to meet the goals of the unit? Be sure that these statements reflect language as it will be used in the real world.

Table 23. Unit Template: Toolbox Components

Language Functions	Key functions identified in the context of how they will be used in the unit or customized from NCSSFL-ACTFL Can-Do Statements
Related Structures	Grammatical structures or sentence patterns required by the function
Vocabulary Expansion	Basic vocabulary topics (Tier 1) related to the unit and more precise vocabulary (Tier 2)
Key Learning Activities/Formative Assessments	A list of major learning experiences
Resources	Specific resources that will be used in the unit
Technology Integration	Suggestions of how learners might work with technology to meet unit goals

Table 24. Unit Template: Toolbox

Toolbox		
Language Functions	**Related Structures/Patterns**	**Vocabulary Expansion**
		Tier 1
Compare *lifestyle routines*	*plus que, moins que, aussi que* (more than, less than, as...as)	expressions/adverbs of frequency sports, activities
		Tier 2
Describe *your daily schedule*	*(le) lundi...*(on Mondays)	*Une bonne hygiène de vie* (a healthy lifestyle)
Ask and answer questions *about daily routines*	interrogative pronouns and adjectives	*Un régime équilibré* (a balanced diet)
Express frequency *saying when and how often you do certain things*	adverbs	*La détente* (relaxation)
Express needs *saying what you need to do to be healthy*	*Il faut/Il me faut* (It's necessary/I need)	*Se détendre/se dépêcher* (to relax/to hurry)
Express opinions *about daily activities, schedules*	*Il est important de, Il est bon de* (It's important to/it's good to)	*Être détendu/être stressé* (to be relaxed/to be stressed)
Make suggestions *about ways to be healthy*	*Tu devrais/Vous devriez, Il te/vous faut* (You should/you need to)	

Related Structures/Patterns. Once the language functions for the unit are in place, the related grammatical structures or language patterns are identified. This is done to make certain that structures and patterns have a communicative purpose, allowing the focus on form to occur within the context of a text. Language learning should never be driven by grammar instruction alone, and language instruction must avoid manipulating grammatical structures out of context. Learners who only know grammar will struggle to be able to use the language in meaningful ways (Shrum & Glisan, 2010). By connecting structures with functions, grammar remains an integral part of language instruction, but it is seen as part of the communicative process. Moeller and Ketsman (2010) discussed the prevailing theories with regard to grammar instruction and reported on various studies that examined best practices on the teaching of grammar. Based on their findings, they then created several activities designed to illustrate the principles of best practice. They recommend that such activities:

- allow learners to complete a task before working in pairs to construct and explain the grammar rule;
- allow learners to see examples of rules in context before being asked to analyze and apply the pattern in a new context; and
- require that learners complete tasks that require them to focus on both form and meaning.

Table 24 shows how the structures/patterns in the Toolbox of the unit template are connected to the language functions. For example, learners need to express frequency, saying how often they do certain activities. In order to be able to do this, they will need to know some adverbs of frequency and will need to know where those adverbs are placed in a sentence.

Vocabulary Expansion. Traditionally, vocabulary was learned from lists and there were often too many words on the list for vocabulary acquisition to take place. Strong learners were able to memorize the words for a test, but often forgot them quickly. Learners seemingly understand the cycle of memorizing and forgetting since it is not uncommon to hear older learners say, "Quick give me the test, before I forget!" These learners had memorized lists of words without being able to use the words in any meaningful context. The days of the week were taught as a list and learners recited and wrote the seven days of the week, scoring well if they knew all seven in the correct order. The communicative approach requires that vocabulary be used in meaningful ways. Today's learners are far more likely to learn to use the days of the week in the context of a communicative function. If learners are trying to find out who has the busier schedule on a certain day in the sample unit, one learner might begin by asking, "What are you doing *on Saturday?*"

The Common Core State Standards comment on vocabulary acquisition and present three tiers of vocabulary that learners encounter in speech and text. Figure 7 summarizes the three tiers.

Figure 7. Three Tiers of Vocabulary Instruction

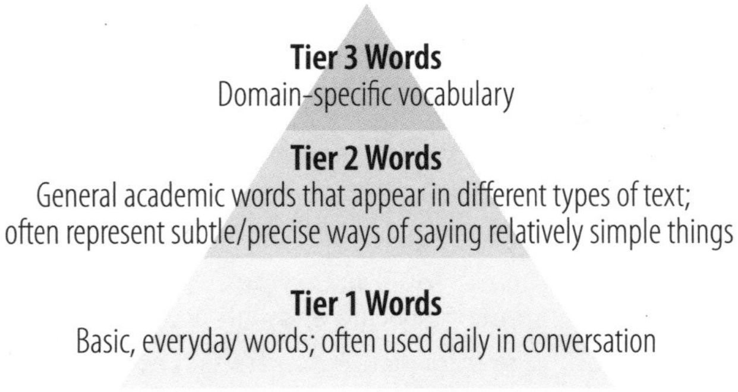

Tier 3 Words
Domain-specific vocabulary

Tier 2 Words
General academic words that appear in different types of text; often represent subtle/precise ways of saying relatively simple things

Tier 1 Words
Basic, everyday words; often used daily in conversation

This model was developed originally by Beck, McKeown, and Kucan, and considers words in terms of how often they occur and how often they are actually used. They acknowledge that the term *tier* may imply a hierarchy or importance, but state that all words are important in terms of comprehension. The difference is often that Tier 2 and Tier 3 words require a more deliberate effort on the part of the teacher and learner due to their relative infrequency of use or domain-specific nature. More importantly, they also acknowledge that Tier 1 words will also require deliberate effort for learners who are acquiring a new language (National Governors Association, 2010, Appendix A, pp. 32–35).

Both Tier 1 and Tier 2 words are important in language classrooms. Learners who are learning a new language lack the Tier 1 vocabulary that is often acquired outside of school through repeated encounters with others and in natural contexts. When determining Tier 1 words, exercise caution and list only the words that are truly relevant to the topic. Many traditional lists are guilty of adding words that are not high frequency and not truly Tier 1 words. For example, the more traditional clothing list often had several items of clothing, but then added descriptive words such as plaid and polka-dot or texture words like wool, cotton, or silk. To narrow the list, imagine how potential Tier 1 words would be used in normal daily conversations. It's easy to imagine hearing a compliment, "I love your skirt. Where did you buy it?" and less likely to think along the lines of, "I love your (plaid) skirt? Is it wool or silk?"

Language learners also need Tier 2 academic language. Terms such as "compare and contrast" are equally important in both English and the target language and such vocabulary is critical as learners advance in proficiency levels. Equally important is the concept that Tier 2 words allow simple things to be expressed in more precise ways. All languages have words and phrases that do not translate easily into other languages. They are terms that convey a precision of meaning and often bring a cultural perspective that is unique to the language. The term *"joie de vivre"* which translates literally as "joy of living" conveys a deeper meaning in French culture that is not easily expressed in English. It is a truly unique French expression and one that is logically a part of a unit that is discussing a balanced lifestyle.

Tier 3 words are domain specific and will be most important as learners work with informational texts as is common in immersion and content-based programs. Learners who might be reading a research piece on sleep would need discipline-specific vocabulary in order to be able to communicate orally and in writing about the topic. However, it is important to remember that Tier 3 words may or may not require mastery, depending on the goals of instruction. They may be part of an article that is being discussed, but are words that may or may not be used frequently outside of the academic setting. The tiered system was created to support teachers as they attempt to determine what words need to be taught, knowing that there will never be enough time to teach all words connected to the topic. Since the amount of vocabulary that can be learned is limited by the amount of time available for the unit and by the age of the learner, be sure that every word that is included is relevant and one that will be used purposefully and frequently during the unit and in other situations. The vocabulary expansion section of the template allows teachers to determine the categories of Tier 1 words that will be part of the unit, but more importantly invites reflection on Tier 2 words that help learners express their ideas more precisely.

> **Pause to consider your unit.** Look carefully at your functions. What grammar or patterns will learners need? For example, in the sample unit, they will need *"Il me faut"* (I need), in order to express need. What Tier 1 words will they need? Are there words and expressions that will allow them to use more precise language? List those Tier 2 words.

Key Learning Activities/Formative Assessments. The template has followed a backward design model allowing teachers to think through the desired results and the acceptable evidence that would serve as proof that learners had achieved the goals of the unit. The final stage of backward design focuses on the learning experiences and instruction that will allow learners to meet the expectations of the unit. Learning experiences are focused and purposeful, formative in nature, and set high expectations (Dougherty, 2012). Both teacher and learners understand the relationship of individual activities in terms of meeting unit goals. Activities that are isolated need to be eliminated or greatly minimized. Workbooks, random textbook activities, homework, worksheets, and quizzes are examples of activities that have the potential to be random and not connected to a unit goal.

Formative assessment is assessment *for* learning. It is an intentional part of instruction that partners teachers and learners in gathering and evaluating evidence of learning in order to improve performance (Moss & Brookhart, 2012). By viewing learning activities as formative assessments, teachers gain valuable information about their instruction and learners receive timely feedback on aspects of their work while there is time to make adjustments. Therefore the unit-planning template does not separate learning activities from formative assessments. Four such activities are shown in Table 2.5, and other activities are described in the complete template (see Appendix H).

Table 25. Unit Template: Learning Activities/Formative Assessments

Learning Activity/Formative Assessment *(representative samples from beginning to end of unit)*	How does this activity support the unit goals or performance tasks?	Mode of Communication	Interculturality **S**elf **C**ommunity **W**orld
Watch video clip of song—*Ma Vie au Soleil* (My Life in the Sun), list activities that relate to *métro, boulot, dodo* (subway, work, sleep) and activities that relate to a more relaxed lifestyle.	Explore elements of a balanced lifestyle	Interpretive	S
Use *Libération* (newspaper) headline and article on stress at school. Have learners complete graphic organizer with statistics from article and then compare to their own situations.	Learn about impact of school on lifestyles	Interpersonal Interpretive	S, C, W
Read article on how French teenagers spend free time. Design survey questions to use with learners studying French. Create graphic organizer to compare school results to those in article. Discuss results in groups.	Explore how French teens spend free-time and make comparisons	Interpersonal Interpretive Presentational	C, W
Work in groups to create a multimedia presentation that explains *métro, boulot, dodo* (subway, work, sleep) in the context of a teenager's life in the United States.	Create a product that explains the lifestyle of a U.S. teenager to French teens	Interpersonal Presentational	C, W

This section of the unit template allows teachers to identify a few key learning activities/formative assessments. The sample activities reflect what teachers might do at the beginning, middle, and end of the unit and they are intentionally grouped to show how learners might work in all three modes to strengthen their language skills. The first column in Table 25 describes the key learning activity/formative assessment with sufficient detail to give a general sense of what might be done. The second column asks for a simple explanation of how the activity supports a learning goal for the unit. The third column asks for the mode(s) of communication that is being used. This column allows teachers to see at a glance that there is a good balance of the interpersonal, interpretive, and presentational modes, but also provides the opportunity to think through ways that an activity might be expanded or reshaped to practice a different mode. Finally, indicate if this is a task that allows the learner to consider the topic from the perspective of self (S), from the perspective of familiar communities (C), or from a global or world perspective (W). Check to see that there is a good balance. Remember that interculturality is the goal and if the indications of community and world are lacking, it may be necessary to reconsider the activities and the materials that anchor the planned activities.

Resources and Technology Integration. It can be challenging to think of resources and technology as the final considerations in unit design, especially if a teacher is moving from a situation where the textbook and accompanying ancillaries and technology pieces have been the curriculum. As you begin the development of a unit, take time to search for resources that will provide a strong foundation for the unit. With your theme and topic in mind and a preliminary essential question, it is critical that you search for authentic resources that will support the unit and inspire your thinking. The song, *Ma Vie au Soleil* (My Life in the Sun), was actually a starting point for the design of this entire unit. It is important to work with authentic materials to the greatest extent possible, recognizing that the textbook is not the curriculum. With an emphasis on authentic texts, the textbook becomes the resource that it was intended to be. Teachers will find appropriate materials in textbooks that support unit goals and textbooks should be mined for those gems. When this is the case, work with your colleagues to determine what is essential and useful from the textbook—opening up opportunities for the use of other materials that support learning goals. Gradually over time you are likely to find that you are using a textbook more as a resource, with authentic texts providing important connections to the real world of native speakers who interact with the same texts. A few resources for the sample unit are listed in Table 26. A detailed resource list and appropriate links are available at www.actfl.org/publications/books-and-brochures/the-keys-planning-learning.

Table 26. Unit Template: Resources and Technology Integration

Resources	Technology Integration
Text for Interpretive Tasks – www3.sympatico.ca/serge.richard2/ www3.sympatico.ca/serge.richard2/page5.html	Teachers can create a safe, free space for learner blogs and more: kidblog.org

Keep in mind that a list of generic resources is not all that helpful. Curriculum documents in the past may have simply listed materials and resources in a generic manner—textbook, workbook, video, songs, etc. Instead, use this section of the template to identify specific instructional resources that will be integral to the unit.

Technology integration is more than just the tools that teachers and learners will use throughout the unit. Technology integration incorporates the definition of literacy from the National Council of Teachers of English referenced earlier, and includes the definition created by the Center for Media Literacy (2011):

> Media Literacy is a 21st century approach to education. It provides a framework to access, analyze, evaluate, create and participate with messages in a variety of forms—from print to video to the Internet. Media literacy builds an understanding of the role of media in society as well as essential skills of inquiry and self-expression necessary for citizens of a democracy (www.medialit.org/media-literacy-definition-and-more).

Technology has made it both easier and more challenging to create content. Computers have certainly allowed writers to write differently. Multiple drafts are possible, material can be copied and pasted, editing programs make proofreading easier, and design programs make it much easier to produce quality final products. Computers now allow for multimedia components to be incorporated, and writers can access a variety of spaces where text can be composed and shared. Tools exist to allow the writing process to be collaborative and interactive. Today's learners must be able to manage and use all of these tools well if they are to create and share content (DeVoss, Eidman-Aadahl, & Hicks, 2010). The unit template includes space to indicate how technology is integrated within the unit. Table 26 suggests an educational site for blogging.

Three sites that share information on current technology tools are listed here and more are available at www.actfl.org/publications/books-and-brochures/the-keys-planning-learning.

- U.S. Digital Literacy—Resource for teachers with annotated information about recommended sites: digitalliteracy.us/best-tools/
- Edudemic—Site that offers complete "how-to" guides on various topics related to teaching and learning: www.edudemic.com/guides/
- NovaSTARTALK—Technology Enhanced Language Instruction—Tools are organized by how the tool would be used: presentation, audio, video, etc. All examples are related to language classrooms: novastartalk.nvcc.edu

> ✅ **Pause to consider your unit.** Identify your resources and consider the role that technology will play in your unit. Consider carefully the text that you will use to launch the unit. Find texts that can be used in a variety of ways. Try to organize the activities in ways that make sense, showing how learners will make progress toward a specific goal.

The Balanced Lifestyle unit is culturally focused and considers personal lifestyles, communities, and world perspectives. It is intrinsically interesting and gives learners the opportunity to focus on their own health and well-being. The performance tasks allow for meaningful communication in each mode and the tasks are cognitively engaging. Learners consider an issue from different perspectives and propose solutions. Finally, it is Standards-based, addressing each of the 5 Cs in a meaningful way. This unit is based on the mindset for effective thematic unit design, providing learners with purposeful and meaningful practice to build their communication skills toward increased proficiency. Remember, proficiency guides all curriculum and unit decisions. In the next chapter, we propose a template for lesson planning to facilitate implementation of the thematic unit on a daily basis.

Application

1. You are convinced that curriculum should be designed around thematic units. What would you say to convince your colleagues who are worried about the change?

2. You are mentoring a young teacher and have just observed a lesson using dated materials that did not appear to be of interest to several learners. How might you use the thematic unit mindset to help her reflect on her lesson?

3. You want to explain the Skills Framework for 21st Century Learning image to a colleague. What would you say? What examples would you share to help her understand the concept of interculturality?

Reflection

1. How did a recent unit of mine address each principle of the thematic unit mindset? Are there changes that I might make when I teach the unit again? Why would I make those changes?

2. How do the units I teach connect to the Global Themes or the AP/IB Themes? How might I use those connections to strengthen my units?

Chapter 3 | Lesson Design

I never teach my pupils; I only attempt to provide the
conditions in which they can learn.

— Albert Einstein

What Does the Teacher Need to Consider to Create a Learner-Centered Classroom?

A teacher may complain that she is working harder than her students. She realizes that she spends hours each week preparing lessons that will engage learners—lessons that are designed to keep learners involved and focused on the objectives. Then, during each class period she acts as the orchestra conductor for the class, directing learners from one activity to the next. At the end of the lesson, the teacher is exhausted and realizes that she had found and created the necessary materials, presented all of the new information, and led the discussions. The challenge for this teacher is to create a more learner-centered classroom. The National Capital Language Resource Center offers the following definition of a learner-centered classroom:

> Learner-centered instruction encourages students to take responsibility for their own language skill development and helps them gain confidence in their ability to learn and use the language. Teachers support students by devoting some class time to non-traditional activities, including teaching learners how to use learning strategies, how to use available tools and resources, and how to reflect on their own learning. (NCLRC, 2003)

In addition to the concepts of self-assessment and reflection that were discussed in the section on LinguaFolio (Chapter 1), the learner-centered classroom requires an understanding of:

- motivation;
- self-efficacy;
- differentiation; and
- brain-based learning and its implications for lesson design.

Motivation. In today's globally connected world, knowing how to communicate in more than one language is a real-world skill. No longer do you have to depend on travel to have the opportunity to meet and converse with someone who speaks a language that is not your own. You can connect with people around the world right from your desktop. Yet even with this "instant access" to speakers of other languages, there is still a need to convince learners, parents, administrators, and community members that the skills that are acquired through learning a language are vital in a world where, according to many Americans' perceptions, everyone speaks English. That mindset of "English is all that I need" reduces motivation or can make it disappear. This is a significant issue because research shows that "motivation is a consistently strong predictor of successful language learning" (coerll.utexas.edu/methods/modules/learners/02/).

In trying to address this issue and understand why people study languages, Gardner and Lambert (1972) identified two types of motivation to learn languages: *instrumental* and *integrative*. Learning a language with the goal of getting a job, getting into college, meeting a graduation requirement, or receiving a promotion is identified as instrumental motivation. The second type of motivation, integrative, is when the learner is personally motivated to learn a language in order to become acquainted with people who speak the language studied and the related culture. Following Gardner and Lambert's work, Graham (1985) identified a third type of motivation: assimilative. In this type of motivation, the learner has a strong desire to become a member of the culture that speaks the language the learner is studying. Pink (2009) also recognizes the importance that motivation plays in learning. He comments that getting an A in French class is simply an achievement or performance goal and one that would be indicative of instrumental motivation. He considers it far more important that learners have learning goals such as the integrative or assimilative goal of learning to speak French in order to meet and become acquainted with people whose native language is French. By placing an emphasis on learning for personal reasons, current learners are more likely to become lifelong learners.

Horowitz (2008) suggests that the types of motivation defined by Gardner and Lambert may not be compelling for everyone, given the attitudes that many Americans have towards learning languages other than English. The following classroom strategies, based on suggestions by Horowitz (2008), may more effectively motivate learners once they are in a world language classroom:

- Help learners set personal goals: identify reasons that are personally relevant to their lives and future plans; set realistic and attainable communication goals facilitated by tools such as LinguaFolio.
- Discuss attitudes about the target language and culture: distinguish between stereotypes and generalizations related to the people who speak the target language; have learners document their experiences with other languages and cultures and the people who speak other languages as evidence of their growing interculturality.
- Connect to native speakers and authentic materials: share a wide variety of authentic materials with learners; introduce learners to native speakers within your community and in locations around the world via technology to make the language "come alive."

Concerning the actual daily routine in a language classroom, the following strategies help create a positive, productive, and pleasant atmosphere, motivating learners to continue their study of another language. These strategies are based on research conducted by Dörnyei and Csizér (1998) and on recommendations made by Shrum and Glisan (2010):

- Conduct the class in the target language, making sure that the language is comprehensible to the learners: use visuals, gestures, acting, facial expressions, props, and drawing, and be ready to repeat, rephrase, simplify, and slow down your speech as needed.
- Encourage learners to use the target language with one another continuously including during unstructured times.
- Share the daily learning objectives at the beginning of class, and refer to them during class as appropriate so that learners know the purpose for the activity or task; check for understanding frequently and adjust plans accordingly, moving more quickly or more slowly as needed.

- Give clear instructions and model how to complete the activity or task successfully.
- Teach learners how to ask for clarification when they don't understand something, using phrases such as: repeat please; I don't understand; slow down please; what does (x) mean; can you explain this (again).
- Create a friendly atmosphere where learners are comfortable taking risks with the language and making mistakes as they try to create meaning with the target language;
- Make pair and small group work part of the regular classroom routine, assigning communicative tasks that are purposeful and meaningful.
- Provide opportunities for learners to help set the agenda concerning what they are learning and how they will demonstrate what they have learned.
- Make learning fun: "The role that fun plays with regard to intrinsic motivation in education is twofold. First, intrinsic motivation promotes the desire for recurrence of the experience . . . Secondly, fun can motivate learners to engage themselves in activities with which they have little or no previous experience" (Bisson & Luckner, 1996).

These factors are critical in terms of building relationships and creating the classroom climate that is essential to building a strong learning community in the classroom.

Self-Efficacy. Self-concept of ability, or self-efficacy, is also important when considering how students learn. Learners need to believe that participation in new learning experiences will lead to success rather than failure. They need to know that they are capable of setting and achieving short-term, realistic goals. The teacher's role is to give learners strategies that allow them to meet their goals. This is critically important, especially for older learners who may have acquired behaviors that cause them to be failure-avoidant rather than success-oriented. When older learners begin to feel that they are not able to do something, they may begin to engage in behaviors to avoid failure—not trying, procrastinating, denying that they tried and reporting false effort, behaviors that are often seen as "failure with honor" (Ames, 1990; Marzano, 2006). Teachers enhance self-efficacy and increase success-oriented behavior when they make certain that learners know what they are supposed to learn and create learning experiences that help learners achieve these goals. Marzano (2006) reports that learners credit their success to four possible attributes—ability, luck, task difficulty, and effort. Learners who believe that ability plays a role in success may be quick to believe that others succeed because they have greater ability. Those who rarely feel success may be too quick to say that they were lucky or that the task was just easy on those occasions when they succeed. Those who attribute their success to individual effort are more likely to see the relationship between their effort and their level of success. Therefore, many learners need help to see the correlation between effort and achievement. Marzano (2006) suggests that learners have the opportunity to reflect frequently on the amount of effort they put into a task and the results they achieve on that task. Creating a cycle of success is critical if learning is to occur, but this does not mean lowering expectations. All learners are expected to meet unit goals and differentiation greatly increases the chance of meeting individual learner needs as they work toward those goals.

Differentiated Instruction. Differentiation means tailoring instruction to meet individual needs. Whether teachers differentiate content, process, products, or the learning environment, the use of ongoing assessment and flexible grouping makes this a successful approach to instruction (Tomlinson, 1999). Based on Tomlinson's suggestions for differentiation, language teachers can differentiate:

CONTENT

- Using a variety of texts on a topic at different levels of complexity;
- Using images to accompany step-by-step instructions;
- Making videos that explain new concepts for learners to view on their own time;
- Providing videos and websites related to the content of the unit;
- Supplying vocabulary lists to accompany interpretive tasks;
- Supplying word banks when completing writing tasks;

PROCESS

- Offering the option for learners to work alone, in pairs or small groups to complete a reading or writing practice assignment;
- Providing help sessions or tutors to work with learners individually or in small groups;
- Leading a "think aloud" to model the steps in reading a text;
- Varying the length of time to work on a task;

PRODUCTS

- Allowing learners to complete a task at their proficiency level;
- Letting learners choose the medium they will use to demonstrate that they have met the unit goal;

LEARNING ENVIRONMENT

- Creating a "help desk" bulletin board with suggestions of websites and other resources to practice the language;
- Organizing the resources in the classroom so that they are easily accessible to all learners;
- Providing quiet space to work without distractions; and
- Providing space for learners to work together in pairs or groups.

Motivation, self-efficacy, and differentiation are key pieces that inform decisions teachers must make about how to best support individual learners. All three require teachers to be thoughtful, recognizing that what applies to one learner is not likely to be true of another. Let's consider one additional factor that cannot be overlooked when planning for learning—the brain. How can we use what we know about how the brain learns to enhance learning?

Application of Brain-Based Learning Principles. Since teachers are trying to facilitate learning, they are in essence trying to change the brain every day. The more they know about how the brain learns, the more successful they can be (Sousa, 2006). Brain research provides insights into how individuals learn, when they are learning best, and their capacity for learning new items. The research also stresses how individuals move information from working memory into long-term memory, providing critical considerations for learning and retention. Careful attention to these concepts can enhance the effectiveness of a lesson and cause more students to meet the learning objectives of the individual lesson.

The brain seeks novelty and an environment that contains mainly predictable or repeated stimuli lowers the brain's interest in the outside world and tempts it to turn within for novel sensations. Lessons that are not cognitively engaging, those that tend to focus only on the lower levels of Bloom's Taxonomy, create an environment that is predictable. Such lessons almost always guarantee that some learners will look for other distractions and these learners are more likely to attempt to text, to daydream, or disrupt others. Teachers who use multisensory activities during a learning episode are more likely to engage the learner, resulting in increased retention of new material (Sousa, 2006). Himmele and Himmele (2011) explain that a total-participation mindset is essential for ensuring high levels of learner engagement and they stress that learning experiences need to be designed to be high cognition and high participation. Teachers who are engaged in facilitating the learner-centered multisensory classroom focus on lesson goals with an emphasis on what learners will do. Learners work in pairs, in groups, or alone depending on the task and the classroom atmosphere is purposeful, noisy, and busy at appropriate times. Learners assess their own learning and both learners and the teacher provide feedback (NCLRC, 2003).

Brain research suggests that teachers pay close attention to the primacy–recency effect which states that individuals learn best what they learn first and last. Therefore, teachers should generally plan to do what is most important at the start of the lesson and should make certain to close lessons in ways that allow learners to consolidate their learning and demonstrate progress toward lesson objectives. Consequently, teachers should limit the amount of input given at one time by opting instead for a cycle of input followed by guided and independent practice. Subsequent cycles allow for additional input followed again by guided and independent practice. Figure 8 suggests what a typical 20-minute cycle might look like in terms of a learning experience for an adolescent or adult.

Figure 8. Primacy–Recency Learning Cycle Adapted from Sousa (2006)

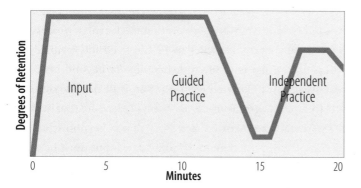

The age of the learner also determines how much information can be processed at one time. Research suggests that the number of minutes involved in the cycle approximates the age of the learner, but a cycle should never last more than 20 minutes. An adolescent or adult can normally process an item in working memory intently for 10 to 20 minutes before mental fatigue or boredom with that item occurs and the individu-

al's focus drifts (Sousa, 2006; Curtain & Dahlberg, 2010). Schmoker (2011) suggests that teachers focus on working with small, ordered steps, allow time for thinking, and practice new learning by talking or writing. This deliberate process respects the limits of memory and average attention span and allows the learner to process the new information every few minutes. The lesson-planning template is designed so that teachers can plan an instructional sequence that is chunked in ways that allow learners to progress in small ordered steps with time to use new information as it might be used in the real world (Sousa, 2006). Figure 8 is intended to be an approximation of a learning cycle that can be helpful when making decisions about how to structure a lesson. However, it would be nearly impossible to follow the cycle minute-by-minute given the need to change and adapt to students' needs during the lesson. As the lesson template is explained, we will explore the implications of this learning cycle in more detail.

Mindset for Lesson Plan Design

What Design Elements Should Be Considered When Planning a Lesson? A good lesson seems effortless, but its success is determined by how carefully a teacher attends to those elements that provide structural support for the lesson while maximizing potential for learning. Three critical factors are:

- 90%+ use of target language;
- comprehensible input; and
- planning for transitions.

90%+ Use of Target Language. Learners come to our classes with an expectation that they will be able to use the language they are learning; our challenge as teachers is to create the classroom environment that will allow this to happen. ACT-FL published a position statement stating that teachers and learners should use the target language at least 90% of the time at all levels of instruction during instructional time and, when feasible, beyond the classroom (ACTFL, July 2012). ACTFL's position statement reflects a well-established position in second language acquisition: Target language input and interaction are essential to acquisition and the development of communicative competencies. By setting the goal at 90% or more, ACTFL's position statement also recognizes that there are times when use of English may be beneficial to the learner (LeLoup, Ponterio, & Warford, 2013).

While the transition to a culture of teaching in the target language may prove to be challenging, it is critical that learners have the opportunity to hear and use the language purposefully throughout the class period. The decision to use English should be a conscious one with a clear pedagogical purpose; experts in the field advocate for judicious use of English to avoid having learners feel that everything of "importance" will be stated in English (Curtain & Dahlberg, 2010). This means that teachers must be careful and systematic about what will be said in English. Limited translation to support comprehension of new vocabulary or structure can have a place, but it cannot be the routine or learners will quickly realize that they can simply wait for the translation (LeLoup et al., 2013).

Adherence to the 90%+ guideline does mean that teachers have a few minutes each day when they can use English if necessary and teachers may want to consider how they and learners will signal a switch from the target language to English. Some use signs designating the language that is to be spoken, others require that both the teacher and learners ask for permission in the target language to use English before switching. Many advocate for using English only to establish lesson objectives posting those Can-Do Statements in English in the room in order to ensure that all learners understand what they are expected to be able to do. As learners advance in proficiency, those objectives are still posted in English for clarity in setting lesson objectives, but may also be posted in the target language. Clementi (in Crouse, 2012) advocates for the use of English outside the classroom to allow learners to explore cultural topics at a deeper cognitive level, so that the resulting target language discussions that occur in class can be held at a simpler linguistic level while still allowing for a deeper understanding of the issue. While it is important to maintain the use of the target language, it is essential that the message be comprehensible if learning is to occur.

Comprehensible Input. Consider how challenging it is to listen to a radio program in a language that you do not understand well. You are a motivated learner and are determined to improve your language skills, but you quickly realize that you are not able to maintain your focus. The same thing is likely to happen when watching a movie in another language. Even the visuals can't hold your attention for long. This also happens when reading a text that is not comprehensible. Learners who encounter any type of text including lectures or comments made by the teacher that are too challenging are likely to give up in frustration. They hold low expectations for themselves, believing that they are incapable of processing the text. These low expectations develop as learners attempt to struggle with a text that is simply too challenging, and then lose interest in the topic due to lack of comprehension. Lent (2012) identifies this as a cycle for failure. Stephen Krashen's Input Hypothesis states that acquisition occurs only when learners receive an optimal quantity of comprehensible input (i+1) (Shrum & Glisan, 2010).

Giving instructions for an activity is one area where teachers may be tempted to resort to English in order to save time and guarantee comprehension. Instead, the teacher may opt to use the target language at a level slightly beyond what learners understand (i+1), but model what is being said by engaging in the activity with a learner in front of the class. Learners are hearing the directions in the target language, but they are also being given visual support to make the language more comprehensible (LeLoup et al., 2013).

As teachers work to make input comprehensible, they need to remember that the key factor is to ascertain that learners can complete the task that accompanies the text. Learners who are able to extract meaning from an authentic text will build confidence in their ability to work with those texts and will create conditions that are similar to the way a child processes his or her first language. A young child rarely understands every word that he/she encounters, but still attends to the message to get the main idea. Teachers may believe that if they revert to translation in an effort to make certain that learners understand everything, they are accelerating the learning process. In fact, this may cause a learner to be hindered in his ability to process a text that is of interest, but slightly beyond his comprehension level. Comprehensible input must not be confused with total comprehension. Even the youngest learner will sit on a parent's lap and listen to a story that is beyond what she can completely comprehend. In summary, input must be comprehensible and it must be meaningful for learning to occur. Teachers can make input more comprehensible by using the visual support, and verbal and nonverbal cues listed in Table 27 (Fortune, 2012).

Table 27. Making Input Comprehensible (Fortune, 2012)

Visual Support	Verbal Cues	Nonverbal Cues
Visuals and props Graphics Realia Pictures Graphic organizers	Exaggerated pronunciation Slower than normal speech Purposeful pauses Intonation or tone of voice Slowed speech for emphasis Key word emphasis and repetition Paraphrasing (saying it in an easier way)	Gestures Facial expressions Pantomime Demonstration Routine Context clues

Lesson Transitions. One additional aspect of lesson planning is the need to manage transitions. There is no way to capture transitions on an actual lesson plan template. They occur at the start and end of class and at times during the lesson when there is a shift in learning experiences. They occur when class is interrupted when the principal comes to the door with a question. The sample lesson plan has six transitions and there could be more depending on adjustments that have to be made during the lesson. Managing those minutes becomes a mindset for teachers, and can be the determining factor in whether a lesson proceeds smoothly or results in too much downtime with the teacher constantly having to bring the learners back to attention. Hunter and Hunter (2004) coined the term "sponge activities" to designate activities that would soak up the wasted minutes that could be used productively for review or reflection. These sponge activities allow teachers to use every available minute to reinforce learning. While it is possible to plan sponge activities that are lesson-specific, it is also possible to work from a set of activities that can be easily adapted to meet any situation. Consider the following activities:

- Answer a question from different perspectives.
- Brainstorm as many words as you can for this image/concept.
- Complete a sentence frame.
- Complete an admit or exit slip.
- Draw and caption a summary.
- Interview your partner to find out (x).
- Provide definitions by using circumlocution.
- Read and identify the most important word or main idea.
- Read and write a title for (x).
- State your opinion of (x).
- Take turns describing (x).
- Think of three things to say about (x).

- Write a tweet that summarizes (x).
- Write a five-word description of the story.
- Write a question for a future quiz.
- Write questions you would like to ask.

Table 28 shows how sponge activities might be used to manage transitions in order to make every available minute count.

Table 28. Transition/Sponge Activities in the Classroom

The teacher says…	Learners:
While I take attendance . . .	write two questions to find out how busy your partner is.
While I pass out the graphic organizer . . .	think of ways to complete the following sentence, "I have fun when I . . ."
While I answer this student's question…	role-play a (30-second) conversation with your partner. If you run out of things to say, start over.
While I find the picture . . .	tweet what you like to do.
We have one minute left . . .	use circumlocution to see how many of the following words you can get your partner to say.

Lesson Plan Design

Backward Design. The lesson plan template that is used here is certainly not the only way to think through the lesson planning process, but it is designed to capture the more important concepts of a well-designed lesson by using the backward design process. Teachers:

- identify desired results by determining the objectives for the lesson;
- determine acceptable evidence and know how individual learners will provide that evidence; and
- plan learning experiences and instruction.

Identify desired results: The objectives for the daily lesson reflect the unit goals. The lesson plan template begins the backward-design process by asking that the teacher refer back to the unit plan to capture critical information. The unit theme and essential question are restated in order to maintain focus on the unit goals.

It can be hard to narrow the focus of a lesson and much easier to list a series of activities that have the potential to capture the interest of the learner. Learners in the classroom of a teacher who plans lessons by simply thinking through a list of activities might see a list such as the one that appears in Figure 9.

Figure 9. List of Activities

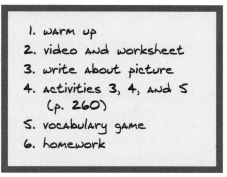

1. warm up
2. video and worksheet
3. write about picture
4. Activities 3, 4, and 5 (p. 260)
5. vocabulary game
6. homework

The agenda conveys the activities for the day, but it fails to state in clear terms what learners will be able to do with the language as a result of those activities. It's not enough to just use the language; the language must be used in ways that allow learners to make progress toward the daily communicative objective. Language teachers may find the following questions to be helpful when creating objectives or identifying desired results:

- Why are you doing this activity? What is the purpose?
- What will learners be able to do as a result of the lesson that they couldn't do at the start of the lesson?
- Does this objective reflect language as it is used in the real-world?

All lessons must have clear learning objectives to ensure that meaningful learning and effective teaching occur. Learners need to know how they will know when they have achieved the daily objective and how they will demonstrate their learning.

Once the daily objectives or Can-Do Statements have been determined, they are:

- posted so that learners can see the objectives throughout the lesson;
- referenced so that learners are continually aware of what they are supposed to be able to do; and
- assessed so that the learners know where they are with regard to the objectives.

Determine acceptable evidence. Planning a lesson requires that teachers think like assessors (Wiggins & McTighe, 1998). As assessors, teachers select activities that allow learners to demonstrate their progress toward specific lesson objectives. Both teachers and learners know how they will measure progress toward those objectives. The following questions may be help-

ful when deciding the type of evidence that will measure individual learning:

- What is sufficient proof that learners are meeting the daily objectives?
- What will I ask learners to do that will provide concrete evidence of who really understands?
- How will each individual learner know that they have met the lesson objective before the end of class?
- What are available tools that can help me document learner progress more precisely and efficiently?

Teachers who design effective lessons make a conscientious effort throughout the lesson to ensure that all learners are progressing in each segment of the lesson before moving on to the next one. The teacher continually conducts formative assessment at each stage of the lesson to see how learners are progressing. Strategies that elicit performance in each mode while checking for understanding include:

Interpretive

- Acting out the sequence of events or scene that is described.
- Identifying and explaining most important word or sentence.
- Signaling—thumbs up/thumbs down, true/false.
- Signaling by using clickers or web-based tools.

Interpersonal

- Calling on a sampling of learners randomly to ask/answer a question.
- Exchanging information in line-up or inner–outer circle.
- Role-playing.
- Using the strategy of think–pair–share, think–write–pair–share.

Presentational

- Completing A–Z word list on topic.
- Completing an exit slip.
- Processing using quick write or quick draw.
- Responding to a question according to an assigned number (numbered-heads-together).
- Responding in a journal.
- Writing responses on dry erase boards.

These constant checks for understanding provide critical feedback to the learner, while allowing teachers to determine what is needed later in the lesson or in subsequent lessons. Learners benefit from lessons that are focused on clear learning objectives and those that are delivered in short instructional "chunks" or segments punctuated by multiple cycles of guided practice and formative assessment. The cycle of guided practice with multiple checks for understanding allows learners to know how well they are meeting lesson objectives (Marzano, 2007; Schmoker 2011). Learners provide evidence of and assess their own learning and are therefore better prepared for subsequent lessons. Refer back to Figure 8 to see how the primacy–recency learning cycle supports the cycle of input, guided practice, and formative assessment.

Plan learning experiences and instruction. Teachers may be tempted to plan by selecting activities with the sole purpose of making class more enjoyable. Injecting an element of fun into a lesson is important, but this must also be purposeful, helping learners build their communication skills. For example, a teacher may decide that she wants learners to work with new vocabulary and decides on a game of bingo or flyswatter. These games are fun and may help learners acquire vocabulary, but they cannot be played in isolation. They need to be connected directly to other activities that ask the learners to use vocabulary that they practiced in the game for meaningful communication. If, during a game, learners practiced vocabulary related to what you see on a street from the target culture, they might work in pairs, each person with a slightly different image of a street scene. They must ask and answer questions about similarities and differences between the images in an information gap activity. Learners use the new vocabulary in a context where that vocabulary might be used in real-life situations and the activities become "minds-on" rather than merely "hands-on." The following questions may be helpful when determining learning experiences:

- How will the activities I've chosen address the lesson objectives?
- Do I have the resources I need to support lesson objectives?
- "What do I know about language learning in general that leads me to believe that my choices will be effective?" (Duncan & Met, 2010, p. 8)

Each lesson is structured so that teachers and learners focus on the daily lesson objective. They require teachers to reflect and consider carefully what the next steps will be to advance learning, while recognizing that not all learners will advance at the same rate.

Planning for Instruction. Table 29 provides a summary of what might occur at each stage of backward design showing that

this teacher has a clear understanding of what learners in her classroom are expected to be able to do by the end of the lesson.

Table 29. Lesson Plan Summary Showing Elements of Backward Design

Lesson Element	Application in lesson:
Daily objectives	Learners can: • name obligations and optional activities that create balance in daily life based on authentic video, *Ma Vie au Soleil* (My Life in the Sun) • ask and answer questions about what they do to create balance in their lives
Learning activities	Learners create an individual chart of obligations and optional activities. They pair to discuss what is on each chart and to determine who has the more balanced lifestyle.
Checks for understanding	Learners work in pairs to classify activities as obligations or optional activities. Individually, learners write simple sentences that convey obligations and optional activities.

The daily objectives are written in terms of what the learner can do. Learners know that they will watch a video and they understand what they are supposed to do as a result of that activity. They understand that they will talk about balance in terms of their lives (identify desired results). Learners will demonstrate comprehension of new vocabulary by classifying expressions and will then write individually about their lives (determine acceptable evidence). Finally, a specific learning experience is described showing how learners will begin to acquire the skills needed (plan learning experiences). There is a clear connection between the activities and the way the teacher is checking for understanding. This lesson vignette also illustrates how formative assessments take place when the learners create individual charts with obligations, pair to discuss the charts, pair to classify the activities, and write simple sentences about those activities. A more detailed lesson plan will be presented later in this chapter.

Lesson Planning. Lesson planning is where theory and good ideas meet the demands of individual learners in the classroom. Each lesson is a carefully sequenced set of tasks designed to allow learners to reach the targeted learning objective of that lesson. Writing a lesson plan is like putting a complicated jigsaw puzzle together. The picture on the box shows you the final result, but the pieces have to be sorted, manipulated, and nudged into place. Teachers might think that they have their plan perfectly organized, but all teachers know that learners have a way of causing a change in plans at any given moment for a multitude of reasons. It is the well-prepared teacher who can easily abandon one plan in favor of another in such a way that learners still meet the targeted objectives.

The Lesson Template

The remainder of this chapter will walk you through the development of a lesson plan. Before continuing to read, you may find it helpful to review the completed lesson plan for A Balanced Lifestyle (Appendix L). You may also wish to print a copy of the blank template (Appendix M). Both templates are also available online at www.actfl.org/publications/books-and-brochures/the-keys-planning-learning. Although it may be tempting to read quickly through the information that is presented here, we believe that it will be more beneficial to read a section for the information and examples that will be provided. Then pause to consider a lesson that you would like to develop and begin to draft that lesson as each component part of the lesson plan is presented here.

The lesson plan template is a tool for organizing thinking. It allows a teacher to identify the learning objective of the lesson, indicating resources and activities that connect clearly to the stated objective. The individual lesson becomes part of the plan for meeting the unit goals. The intent of such a plan is to allow teachers to develop a way of thinking that will support student learning. The sample lesson plan presented here is reflective of how a busy teacher might complete the template. There is enough detail for that teacher, but perhaps not for someone else.

The first fields in the lesson plan template included in this publication are designed to provide an overview to the lesson and to place the lesson in the context of a specific unit. Lesson planning begins when the objectives for the lesson are written. Teachers have a great deal of flexibility when determining how learners will reach those objectives. The lesson objectives may come directly from the unit goals, or teachers may find it necessary to unpack the unit goals by creating more manageable steps. Each lesson has clear communicative and cultural objectives in one or more of the modes of communication. Those objectives allow for the integration of the other goal areas—Connections, Comparisons, and Communities.

The sample lesson plan shown here is for the second day of the unit A Balanced Lifestyle. The first day of any given unit is designed to hook the learners, to frame the unit, and increase student interest in the topic. Day 1 of this unit might focus on headlines that deal with quality of life or with short media clips conveying information about lifestyle balance. Learners may complete a quick poll to determine the percentage of the class who feel stressed before looking at data on the number of teens from other countries reporting that they feel stressed. Using the first day of a unit in this way also allows a teacher to activate prior knowledge and allows learners to make connections to what they are learning in other disciplines. It can also be a day where learners generate questions addressing topics of interest to them.

Remember the goals for the unit A Balanced Lifestyle. Learners will be able to:

- explore health and wellness websites to identify elements of a balanced lifestyle here and in (country in the French-speaking world);
- compare lifestyles of teenagers to those of teenagers in (country in the French-speaking world) in terms of balance;
- make recommendations for ways to create or maintain a balanced lifestyle; and
- create a presentation for (the community) highlighting ways to promote a balanced lifestyle.

Begin by connecting the lesson plan to the unit plan, keeping the goals of the unit in mind as you plan individual lessons. Table 30 shows how information is restated from the unit plan and identifies the specific Can-Do Statement(s) that will serve as lesson objectives.

Table 30. Connecting Lesson Plan to Unit Plan

Language Level: Novice Mid–Novice High	Grade: 9–12		Date: xx	Day in Unit: 2	Minutes: 55
Unit Theme and Question	**Well-Being:** A Balanced Lifestyle *How do people here and in (the French-speaking world) describe a balanced lifestyle?*				
Daily Topic:	*métro, boulot, dodo* (subway, work, sleep)				
STANDARDS	**LESSON OBJECTIVES**				
What are the communicative and cultural objectives for the lesson?	**Communication and Cultures**	*Which modes of communication will be addressed?* ✔ Interpersonal ✔ Interpretive ☐ Presentational	**Learners can:** • Name obligations and activities that create balance in daily life based on authentic video *Ma Vie au Soleil* (My Life in the Sun) • Ask and answer questions about what they do to create balance in their lives		
If applicable, indicate how Connections/Comparisons/Communities/Common Core will be part of your lesson.	**Connections**				
	Comparisons	Language: *métro, boulot, dodo* (subway, work, sleep)			
	Communities				
	Common Core	**Speaking and Listening (SL1):** Prepare for and participate effectively in a range of conversations and collaborations with diverse partners, building on others' ideas and expressing their own clearly and persuasively.			

> ✓ **Pause to consider your lesson plan.** Complete the fields that come from the unit plan. What are the lesson objectives? Do they reflect how learners will use language beyond the classroom? How does this lesson connect to other standards? You may find it easier to return to certain fields as you plan the lesson details.

Gain Attention/Activate Prior Knowledge. Begin by presenting and posting the daily objectives so that learners know what they are expected to be able to do by the end of the lesson. Posting the daily objectives in English ensures that all learners clearly understand the objectives. Ideally, the answer to the common question—"What did you do in class today?" would be "I learned to . . . ." and learners would restate a version of the objectives.

The first few minutes of a lesson are critical in terms of how learners will engage. The primacy–recency cycle is shown again in Figure 10 as a reminder that learners learn best what happens first. Figure 10 also shows the connections between the stages of the lesson plan template and the primacy–recency learning cycle by giving an indication of the amount of time that would ideally be spent on each part of the lesson. This is a learning cycle that can be repeated multiple times within a lesson depending on the length of the lesson. The sample lesson is for a 55-minute class and two learning cycles will be presented for this particular lesson.

Figure 10. Primacy–Recency and Connection to Gain Attention/Activate Prior Knowledge, Provide Input, and Elicit Performance and Provide Feedback

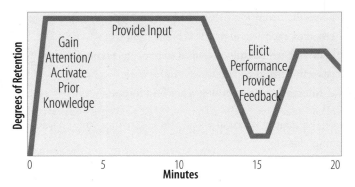

Research on how the brain processes information indicates that only a small portion of the stimuli the brain encounters is actually processed since the reticular activating system (RAS) allows less than 1% of the sensory information to enter the brain every second. This means that teachers must strive to capture or "hook" the learner's attention using the opening activity or "warm-up" to set the stage for what will follow. Table 31 reminds readers of the lesson objectives for the day and shows how this lesson is designed to gain the attention of the learners while activating prior knowledge. Lesson activities are written primarily in terms of what learners will do, there is an indication of how long the activity might take and finally the materials needed are listed.

Table 31. Lesson Objectives and Gain Attention/Activate Prior Knowledge

Learners can:	• Name obligations and activities that create balance in daily life based on authentic video *Ma Vie au Soleil* (My Life in the Sun) • Ask and answer questions about what they do to create balance in their lives		
Lesson Sequence	**Activity/Activities** What will learners do? What does the teacher do?	**Time** How many minutes will this segment take?	**Materials/Resources/Technology** Be specific. What materials will you develop? What materials will you bring in from other sources?
Gain Attention/ Activate Prior Knowledge	Teacher displays a variety of images depicting wellness and stress. Learners look at the images and list activities that they consider to be chores or obligations as well as those that are done by choice or are of interest.	5	Images depicting wellness/stress Images of various activities, preferably images that learners have used in previous units

The lesson for Day 2 of A Balanced Lifestyle begins with images designed to capture the interest of the learners. Prior knowledge is activated when learners generate previously learned vocabulary that connects in some way to those images. As learners become invested in the images and react to the activities, they are more likely to pay close attention since the material is meaningful to them (Willis, 2006). Because the first few minutes of class are so important, it can be helpful to remember to begin class with an activity that:

- gains the attention of the learner;
- engages each learner;
- is doable and achievable as a warm-up, takes no more than five minutes; and
- connects in some way to what will happen next.

Since the beginning of class is prime learning time, avoid beginning class by:

- collecting or checking homework;
- holding individual conferences with learners while other learners wait to begin;
- passing back papers while learners settle in and talk; or
- starting a class with administrative duties.

The warm-up activity sets the stage for what follows and learners will use the images and the vocabulary that they have generated in other parts of the lesson. This ensures that the working memory of learners is not overloaded prior to the introduction of new material (Sousa, 2006).

Cycle 1: Provide Input. The primacy–recency cycle in Figure 10 shows where learners learn best and it is where teachers should do what they believe to be most important. Teachers may find it helpful to ask the question, "What is the most important thing that I intend to do today to enhance learning?" The activities selected for this part of the lesson reflect the answer to that question.

Comprehensible input is key to developing language skills and authentic text is usually the best source for that input. Unfortunately, teachers may dismiss authentic text because they think it is too hard. Consider choosing a book for a young child. Imagine that the child has a deep interest in dinosaurs even though he/she is not yet reading. You would not pick up a book only to set it aside because the vocabulary was too complex or because a certain grammar structure appeared in the text. Instead, you would select a text that is interesting and use a variety of strategies to make the information comprehensible. Find texts that allow learners to be immersed in the language by listening, reading, and/or viewing. Select texts that are intrinsically interesting, cognitively engaging, culturally connected, and communicatively purposeful. Look for an authentic text that is accessible to the learners, but do not have an expectation that learners need to understand everything. The key is to modify the task. The sample lesson plan incorporates the video *Ma Vie au Soleil* (My Life in the Sun) by Keen'v to introduce the theme of the unit. Learners see a businessman who is tired of work and abandons that lifestyle in favor of life on an island. Table 32 adds details on what teachers and learners do during the input part of the lesson.

Table 32. Lesson Objectives, Gain Attention/Activate Prior Knowledge and Provide Input

Learners can:	• Name obligations and activities that create balance in daily life based on authentic video *Ma Vie au Soleil* (My Life in the Sun) • Ask and answer questions about what they do to create balance in their lives		
Gain Attention/ Activate Prior Knowledge	• Teacher shows a variety of images depicting wellness and stress • Learners list activities that they consider to be chores or obligations as well as those that are done by choice or are of interest.	5	• Images depicting wellness/stress • Images of various activities, preferably images that learners have used in previous units
Provide Input	• Learners are given a set of statements concerning the video content. • The teacher reads each statement taking time to develop comprehension. • Learners are asked if they agree or disagree with the statements. • Learners are asked to find proof for or against each statement as they work with the video. The video is shown first with no sound.. Learners have time to individually note proof for and against based on visual images. • Learners also list any words that they expect to hear in the video.	10	• Video *Ma Vie au Soleil* (My Life in the Sun) • Proof for/proof against activity page.

Learners will watch the video for the first time without any sound. They will consider what they see in terms of the proof for/proof against statements that they have discussed before seeing the video. Based on what they see, they will note proof for and against each statement and will also make note of any vocabulary that they believe they will hear when the video is played with the sound.

Cycle 1: Elicit Performance/Provide Feedback. Learners need time to process and apply the information that was shared during the input part of the lesson. A key feature of effective lessons is the conscientious effort that is made by the teacher throughout the lesson to ensure that all learners are learning each segment of the lesson before moving on to the next segment. As learners practice, the teacher conducts formative assessment by checking to see that learners have learned a particular step (Schmoker, 2011). This segment of the lesson plan is designed to allow learners to apply what they are learning in meaningful ways. As learners process new learning, teachers monitor and provide feedback on individual performance. Input followed by performance and feedback creates a cycle of guided practice and checking for understanding (Marzano 2007). Practice is likely to be more effective if teachers plan for strategies that allow learners to demonstrate individual learning. The following questions may be helpful when selecting activities:

• Does the activity ask each individual learner to contribute equally?
• Is there a way to assess individual learner performance at the end of the activity or by the end of the lesson?

• In the interpretive mode, do learners have a guided task to complete as they read, listen or view individually and silently?
• In the interpersonal mode, are learners given the opportunity to speak or write without rehearsing?
• In the presentational mode, do learners have the chance to write their own thoughts before and/or after sharing with others?

At this stage of the lesson the teacher has presented a small amount of material, allowing the learners to think and process that material individually before working with a partner to extend their learning by talking and writing about the new material. The focus is off the teacher and on what learners are able to do with the language. The teacher has a chance to gauge where learners are and what they may need before the next step in the lesson. This mid-lesson feedback is critical since it allows learners to work to achieve the lesson objective and then to receive information that lets them know if they are on track or need to make adjustments. With clear objectives, learners are more likely to seek and listen to feedback: They will know what they know and what they don't know (Brookhart, 2012; Hattie, 2012; Wiggins, 2012). In summary, effective lessons incorporate small, ordered steps; periodic thinking reviews; and practice by talking or writing. Table 33 adds details about what teachers do to elicit performance so the learner can receive feedback on that performance.

Table 33. Lesson Objectives, Gain Attention/Activate Prior Knowledge, Provide Input, Elicit Performance and Provide Feedback

Learners can:	• Name obligations and activities that create balance in daily life based on authentic video *Ma Vie au Soleil* (My Life in the Sun) • Ask and answer questions about what they do to create balance in their lives		
Gain Attention/ Activate Prior Knowledge	• Teacher displays a variety of images depicting wellness and stress • Learners list activities that they consider to be chores or obligations as well as those that are done by choice or are of interest.	5	• Images depicting wellness/stress • Images of various activities, preferably images that learners have used in previous units
Provide Input	• Learners are given a set of statements concerning the video content. • The teacher reads each statement, taking time to develop comprehension. • Learners are asked if they agree or disagree with the statements. • Learners are asked to find proof for or against each statement as they work with the video. The video is shown first with no sound. Learners have time to individually note proof for and against based on visual images. • Learners also list any words that they expect to hear in the video.	10	• Video *Ma Vie au Soleil* (My Life in the Sun) • Proof for/proof against activity page.
Elicit Performance/ Provide Feedback	• Learners indicate by signaling thumbs up or down if they have proof for or against each statement after watching the video. • They pair to share their comments on proof for/against statements. They compare their ideas with their partner's and each adds details to their individual lists. • The teacher asks two or three students to share their responses and then calls on volunteers. • The teacher then asks learners to share words or phrases that they anticipate hearing in the video based on what they saw.	10	

Learners have only seen the video without sound at this point in the lesson. The teacher does a quick thumbs up/thumbs down to see if learners have found proof for or against the statements that were presented before seeing the video. Before sharing as a whole class, learners work with partners to compare results and exchange evidence for and against based on what was seen in the video. The teacher first asks a few students who did not volunteer and then a few students who volunteer, asking them all to share their evidence in support for or against each statement. Finally, the teacher asks students to share words and phrases that they expect to hear in the video.

> ✔ **Pause to consider your lesson plan.** How will you start the lesson? What is most important in terms of lesson objectives? What will learners do to work with the new material? How will you structure an activity to allow for feedback?

The first learning cycle—gaining attention/activating prior knowledge, providing input, eliciting performance, and providing feedback has been completed at this point in the lesson. Since this is a 55-minute class, there is time for an additional learning cycle that begins with another opportunity for input. It's not necessary to repeat the "gain attention" aspect of the lesson, but this is often accomplished by changing the type of work that learners will do.

Cycle 2: Provide Input. The lesson template continues with a second cycle of input, performance, and feedback. In this lesson, learners will again work in the interpretive mode initially, but will then move to the interpersonal mode to discuss personal opinions. After seeing the video for the second time, there is a short period of direct instruction that connects to the objective of the lesson. Direct instruction is still a critical component of a lesson when a teacher needs to present new information. This lesson template allows for direct instruction, but also recognizes the need to pause frequently to allow learners to process and use the new information in meaningful ways. Table 34 describes the second cycle for input.

Table 34. Second Cycle of Input

Learners can:	• Name obligations and activities that create balance in daily life based on authentic video *Ma Vie au Soleil* (My Life in the Sun) • Ask and answer questions about what they do to create balance in their lives		
Provide Input	• The teacher introduces the concept of *métro, boulot, dodo* (subway, work, sleep). • Learners watch the video for a second time with sound on identifying words on their lists that connect to the concept of going to work or working. • The teacher shares a prepared list of activities, drawing from those in the video and from those suggested by students during the warm-up. Learners review and learn new sentence and question frames—What do you do? I do/don't…Do you like…? I like/don't like, Do you want? I want/don't want, Do you have to…? I have to/don't have to—while working with the list of activities.	10	• Images depicting *métro, boulot, dodo* (subway, work, sleep) • Prepared list of activities based on video

Table 35. Second Cycle of Input, Performance, and Feedback

Learners can:	• Name obligations and activities that create balance in daily life based on authentic video *Ma Vie au Soleil* (My Life in the Sun) • Ask and answer questions about what they do to create balance in their lives		
Elicit Performance/ Provide Feedback	• Learners work individually to complete a graphic organizer, writing simple sentences about things they do that relate to the routine of work and things they do for fun. • Learners pair and rotate in inner–outer circles to see what they have in common	10	• Graphic organizer—work, fun and overlap for both

The teacher begins the second input cycle by explaining the concept of "*métro, boulot, dodo*" (subway, work, sleep) using visual images. The learners then watch the video with sound and make note of words on the lists they created earlier in the lesson that relate to the concept of work. The teacher then introduces sentence and question frames that learners will use to discuss what they do. They will discuss the activities that they worked with at the beginning of class by asking and responding to questions about what they like, want, and have to do.

Cycle 2: Elicit Performance/Provide Feedback. It is important that the second input stage is followed by another opportunity for learners to again have a chance to apply what they are learning while receiving feedback. Table 35 shows how learners will demonstrate their understanding of the new material.

Learners work individually to complete a graphic organizer stating what they do for fun and for work. They then have the opportunity to move forming inner–outer circles so that they can rotate and discuss their activities using newly acquired question-and-answer patterns with random partners.

✅ **Pause to consider your lesson plan.** What additional input do learners need? How will they use what they are learning? How will you monitor learning and provide feedback?

Assess Performance/Closure. The teacher was able to assess learner performance on the second objective of the lesson during the inner–outer circle discussions. That discussion activity provided an opportunity for formative assessment on the daily objective: "Ask and answer questions about what they do to create balance in their lives." As learners engaged with multiple partners, the teacher had the opportunity to help individuals or to listen for common problems that could be addressed in the next lesson. The last part of the lesson is designed to capture information on how well each individual student has met the first objective of the lesson. Table 36 shows the closure activity that requires learners to write words and phrases that they associate with an image.

In the last few minutes of class, learners are asked to write any words, phrases, or sentences that they associate with the visual that was shared earlier depicting, "*métro, boulot, dodo*" (subway, work, sleep). These exit slips are collected from each learner, allowing the teacher to see who has met the

Table 36. Lesson Closure

Learners can:	• Name obligations and activities that create balance in daily life based on authentic video *Ma Vie au Soleil* (My Life in the Sun) • Ask and answer questions about what they do to create balance in their lives		
Closure	• Learners are given an image of *métro, boulot, dodo* (subway, work, sleep). They write down any words or sentences that they associate with the images. These are collected and may be used as future prompts for discussion.	10	• Image representative of *métro, boulot, dodo* (subway, work, sleep)

Table 37. Enhance Retention and Transfer

Learners can:	• Name obligations and activities that create balance in daily life based on authentic video *Ma Vie au Soleil* (My Life in the Sun) • Ask and answer questions about what they do to create balance in their lives		
Enhance Retention & Transfer	• Consider the balance in your life. Take the online quiz—test your stress smarts. Consider how you might comment on your results in French in class. • Alternatively, read part of the online article about the health and well-being of teens around the world. Consider how you might share some of what you learned in French in class.		• Articles or references in English or French to enhance awareness of the importance of a balanced lifestyle

daily objective: "Name obligations and activities that create balance in daily life."

Enhance Retention and Transfer. It's important to remember that homework is actually an opportunity for formative assessment. It allows learners to demonstrate that they are able to apply what they have learned in class. Since teachers have been assessing and monitoring learner performance throughout class, they need to decide near the end of the lesson what learners could do to reinforce and possibly extend the objectives of the lesson. Vatterott (2009) explains that there are four purposes for homework: pre-learning, checking for understanding, practice, or processing. When homework is given as a pre-learning activity, the work serves to introduce the topic or may be given to stimulate interest in the topic. It may be used to find out what learners already know and may invite learners to create questions that they have about the topic. Checking for understanding is a valuable way to gauge learning and is a critical step before learners move to practice. Practice has traditionally been the most common reason for giving homework; learners are required to apply what they are learning by practicing rote skills. There is danger in this type of homework if it is assigned before the teacher has proof that learners understand the new learning. Learners may become frustrated and fail to complete the homework or they may complete the homework following an incorrect pattern. The repetition of an incorrect answer

may cause students to "learn" that answer as though it were a correct response. Finally, processing homework allows learners to extend their learning in new ways. Learners apply what they have learned to new situations. Often this type of work is a short- or long-term project, which may be the presentational performance assessment task for the standards-based unit. Table 37 gives two options for extending learning.

The sample lesson plan uses homework as a pre-learning activity by suggesting that learners do some reading in English in order to have a better understanding of the issues that relate to a balanced lifestyle. They will take a personal stress test and are asked to consider comparisons on the health and well-being of teens from around the world. As teachers strive to use the target language at least 90% of the time in class, there is a need to find ways to engage learners at higher cognitive levels when dealing with topics that may be new to them. There is also a need to find ways to allow learners to explore content and culture at the appropriate cognitive level. Using English outside of the classroom is one way to meet this goal. Learners are being given the chance to enhance their understanding of the topic by accessing information in English at home. They are taking responsibility for their own learning and are doing work that may have previously been done in class, thus increasing the amount of class time that is available for interaction with peers in the target language. This type of assignment meets tenets of the flipped classroom (Bergmann, Overmyer, & Wilie, 2012). Alternatively, learners could have been asked to apply what they learned during the lesson by using the target language to:

- check for understanding by expanding the visual representation of *métro, boulot, dodo* (subway, work, sleep) adding words and/or images that captured elements of their personal lifestyle;
- practice by working with the graphic organizer started during class and using that information to create sentences describing their work-related and fun activities; or
- process by writing questions they might ask on a future survey to determine how balanced the lifestyles of their peers in another country are.

> ✓ **Pause to consider your lesson plan.** What information do you need to assess learning? How will learners know that they have met the daily objectives? Is there an extension activity that learners will do at home?

Reflection/Notes to Self. Teachers encounter numerous decision points as they plan and deliver lessons. Danielson (2009) points out that many decisions teachers make become routine and that those decisions are made quickly and automatically based on previous experience. She also states that there are other times when teachers benefit from the opportunity to step back and self-reflect in order to address more substantive issues. It would be impossible to reflect on all of the questions that follow for each lesson. Instead, select those questions that seem most appropriate in order to develop the habit of reflection or draft a question that captures what you want to focus on in any given lesson.

- What worked well? What didn't work? How do you know?
- How would you adapt this lesson or how did you adapt this lesson during the day if it was taught more than once? Why would you make or did you make those changes?
- Did all learners learn? How do you know? What will you do to adapt for those who are not learning?
- Consider some of the key factors in lesson planning as you reflect on/revise the lesson. How was the lesson:
  - goal focused?
  - learner-centered?
  - brain-based?

- How did the lesson provide opportunities for:
  - critical thinking and problem solving?
  - creativity?
  - collaboration?
  - communication?
  - assessment/feedback?
- How was this lesson part of a unit that is:
  - communicatively purposeful?
  - culturally focused?
  - intrinsically interesting?
  - cognitively engaging?
  - standards-based?

The Busy Teacher's Planbook

Teachers have very limited time to write such detailed lessons on a consistent basis, but all teachers benefit by engaging in the process from time to time. Detailed planning makes the process more routine and allows teachers to create their own shorthand that conveys a powerful lesson in a few words. Figure 11 shows what might appear in the lesson plan book of an experienced teacher. When asked for detail, this teacher would be able to give an incredible amount of detail, explaining all that went into the design of what looks to be a simple plan.

Figure 11. Teacher Plan Book

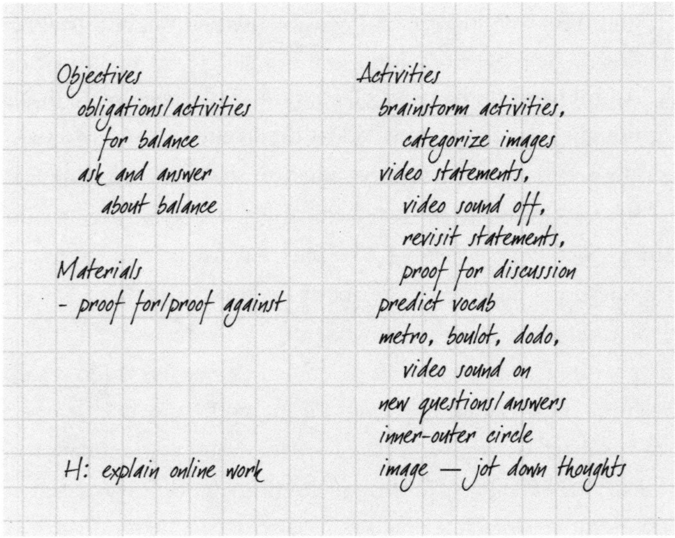

Additional Sample Lesson Plan

A lesson titled Agriculture in China's Regions is part of a unit guided by the question: "How does where I live influence what I eat?" The lesson allows learners to communicate primarily in the interpersonal mode as they focus on the regions and agricultural products found in China. It is an example from a series of 30-minute lessons written for a third grade classroom with novice learners and we have included it here to give an example of how this template might apply to an elementary content-related classroom. Notice that with the shorter class period, there is only one learning cycle of gain attention, provide input, elicit performance, and provide feedback (see Appendix N).

Each day, teachers interact with learners as individuals, manage the classroom, design learning experiences that allow learners to meet lesson objectives, and devise strategies that allow for feedback. Most teachers are thinking constantly, making countless instructional decisions throughout the lesson. The lesson plan template presented in this chapter is designed to help busy teachers organize their lessons in ways that help all learners achieve the lesson objectives. In Chapter 4, we will discuss assessment *of* and *for* learning.

Application

1. A new teacher has come to you concerned because she is always running out of time to finish her lesson plan. What questions would you ask? What strategies might you suggest to help her out?
2. Administration has just asked that all teachers avoid doing homework-related activities at the beginning and end of class. What information would you share with colleagues who are resistant to this change?

Reflection

1. What am I doing to promote learning goals that address integrative or assimilative motivation? How am I dealing with learners who say they are taking the class because it is required for college?
2. What are the benefits of applying the primacy–recency learning cycle in my lessons?
3. What aspects of the lesson-planning template do I consider when planning lessons?
4. How might I use some of the strategies presented in this chapter to involve learners more in the learning process, thus making the class more learner-centered?

Chapter 4 | Assessment of and for Learning

Self-assessment is essential for progress as a learner; for understanding of selves as learners, for an increasingly complex understanding of tasks and learning goals, and for strategic knowledge of how to go about improving.

— *D.R. Sadler*

How Do We Document and Assess Learning in the 21st Century Language Classroom?

With curriculum and instruction aligned to the overarching goal of building learners' proficiency and interculturality, assessments of and for learning must also be aligned with this goal. Performance assessments must be designed with the mindset that these assessments provide evidence of the learner's progress in understanding and communicating respectfully in the target language. Learners need clear criteria that describe the qualities of excellent performance on the task to be assessed. Wiggins and McTighe define assessment in *Understanding by Design Expanded 2nd Edition* (2005): "Assessment is the giving and using of feedback against standards to enable improvement and the meeting of goals" (p. 6).

The ACTFL Proficiency Guidelines and ACTFL Performance Descriptors for Language Learners provide the frameworks for assessing language learning. Figure 12 (previously shown as Figure 3) reintroduces the context for language use and illustrates the difference between performance and proficiency.

Figure 12. Contexts for Performance and Proficiency

Performance
Based on instruction;
familiar content

Proficiency
Independent of instruction;
broad content

As described in Chapter 1, the image on the left shows a school, reminding us that Performance Descriptors describe what learners can demonstrate based on what they have learned and practiced in a more linguistically constrained and supportive instructional setting. Performance is based on familiar contexts and content areas (ACTFL, 2012b). On the right is an image of the Eiffel Tower in Paris, a reminder that Proficiency Guidelines describe what learners can do regardless of where, when, or how the language was acquired and is not limited to the content or curriculum of a particular course (ACTFL, 2012b, pp. 4–5). In the classroom, teachers and learners are constantly working ***toward*** proficiency. It is important to keep the descriptors of the various levels of proficiency in mind when planning lessons, units, and broad curriculum goals for a course or program. Proficiency guidelines serve as the pathway of growth in communication skills for language learners. The ACTFL Proficiency Triangle (Figure 13) visually represents this pathway showing how, as learners move from Novice to Superior levels of proficiency, the pathway widens to accommodate the increasing number of topics that the learners can discuss and the increasing complexity of the language.

Figure 13. ACTFL Proficiency Levels
Levels Are Defined by Tasks

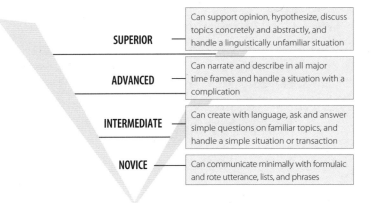

Novice learners use words, phrases, and short memorized sentences and questions to communicate about very familiar topics. Intermediate learners begin to create with language, expressing their thoughts and ideas in strings of sentences; they gradually increase the number of topics they can discuss and the amount of detail they can provide. Advanced learners are "storytellers" as they express their ideas and provide rich details in paragraph-length narration. Although the Proficiency Guidelines include Superior and Distinguished levels, for the purposes of this publication, we are focusing on Novice, Intermediate, and Advanced levels of proficiency.

Targeting Proficiency with Performance in the Classroom

ACTFL Proficiency Guidelines in the Classroom: NCSSFL-ACTFL Global Can-Do Benchmarks. The ACTFL Proficiency Guidelines provide a detailed explanation of what a language user can do in unrehearsed situations at each proficiency level regardless of where, when, or how they learned the target language. The NCSSFL-ACTFL Global Can-Do Benchmarks align with the ACTFL Proficiency Guidelines, but are written in language that is accessible to learners. These statements convey what learners can understand and produce in the language they are learning at the Novice, Intermediate, Advanced, Superior, and Distinguished levels in the interpersonal, interpretive, and presentational modes of communication. Learners should become familiar with this document as they begin their sequence of language study because it will be useful to them for setting personal goals related to what they want to be able to understand and say in the language they are learning. The document also serves as a self-assessment of progress toward achieving those goals. Learners need to be aware of this progression in order to have reasonable expectations as they build their communication skills in the language they are learning. Learners need to understand that learning a language is like learning to play a musical instrument or a sport. It takes time and consistent, meaningful practice to improve. Teachers may find this document useful when working with parents and administrators since it makes clear how the skills of listening, speaking, reading, writing, and two-way interactions develop over time. Table 38 shows the NCSSFL-ACTFL Global Can-Do Benchmarks (See also Appendix F).

Table 38. NCSSFL-ACTFL Global Can-Do Benchmarks

Level/Mode	Interpersonal Communication	Presentational Speaking	Presentational Writing	Interpretive Listening	Interpretive Reading
Novice Low	I can communicate on some very familiar topics using single words and phrases that I have practiced and memorized.	I can present information about myself and some other very familiar topics using single words or memorized phrases.	I can copy some familiar words, characters, or phrases.	I can recognize a few memorized words and phrases when I hear them spoken.	I can recognize a few letters or characters. I can identify a few memorized words and phrases when I read.
Novice Mid	I can communicate on very familiar topics using a variety of words and phrases that I have practiced and memorized.	I can present information about myself and some other very familiar topics using a variety of words, phrases, and memorized expressions.	I can write lists and memorized phrases on familiar topics.	I can recognize some familiar words and phrases when I hear them spoken.	I can recognize some letters or characters. I can understand some learned or memorized words and phrases when I read.

Table 38. NCSSFL-ACTFL Global Can-Do Benchmarks (continued)

Level/Mode	Interpersonal Communication	Presentational Speaking	Presentational Writing	Interpretive Listening	Interpretive Reading
Novice High	I can communicate and exchange information about familiar topics using phrases and simple sentences, sometimes supported by memorized language. I can usually handle short social interactions in everyday situations by asking and answering simple questions.	I can present basic information on familiar topics using language I have practiced using phrases and simple sentences.	I can write short messages and notes on familiar topics related to everyday life.	I can often understand words, phrases, and simple sentences related to everyday life. I can recognize pieces of information and sometimes understand the main topic of what is being said.	I can understand familiar words, phrases, and sentences within short and simple texts related to everyday life. I can sometimes understand the main idea of what I have read.
Intermediate Low	I can participate in conversations on a number of familiar topics using simple sentences. I can handle short social interactions in everyday situations by asking and answering simple questions.	I can present information on most familiar topics using a series of simple sentences.	I can write briefly about most familiar topics and present information using a series of simple sentences.	I can understand the main idea in short, simple messages and presentations on familiar topics. I can understand the main idea of simple conversations that I overhear.	I can understand the main idea of short and simple texts when the topic is familiar.
Intermediate Mid	I can participate in conversations on familiar topics using sentences and series of sentences. I can handle short social interactions in everyday situations by asking and answering a variety of questions. I can usually say what I want to say about myself and my everyday life.	I can make presentations on a wide variety of familiar topics using connected sentences.	I can write on a wide variety of familiar topics using connected sentences.	I can understand the main idea in messages and presentations on a variety of topics related to everyday life and personal interests and studies. I can understand the main idea in conversations that I overhear.	I can understand the main idea of texts related to everyday life and personal interests or studies.
Intermediate High	I can participate with ease and confidence in conversations on familiar topics. I can usually talk about events and experiences in various time frames. I can usually describe people, places, and things. I can handle social interactions in everyday situations, sometimes even when there is an unexpected complication.	I can make presentations in a generally organized way on school, work, and community topics, and on topics I have researched. I can make presentations on some events and experiences in various time frames.	I can write on topics related to school, work, and community in a generally organized way. I can write some simple paragraphs about events and experiences in various time frames.	I can easily understand the main idea in messages and presentations on a variety of topics related to everyday life and personal interests and studies. I can usually understand a few details of what I overhear in conversations, even when something unexpected is expressed. I can sometimes follow what I hear about events and experiences in various time frames.	I can easily understand the main idea of texts related to everyday life, personal interests, and studies. I can sometimes follow stories and descriptions about events and experiences in various time frames.
Advanced Low	I can participate in conversations about familiar topics that go beyond my everyday life. I can talk in an organized way and with some detail about events and experiences in various time frames. I can describe people, places, and things in an organized way and with some detail. I can handle a familiar situation with an unexpected complication.	I can deliver organized presentations appropriate to my audience on a variety of topics. I can present information about events and experiences in various time frames.	I can write on general interest, academic, and professional topics. I can write organized paragraphs about events and experiences in various time frames.	I can understand the main idea and some supporting details in organized speech on a variety of topics of personal and general interest. I can follow stories and descriptions of some length and in various time frames. I can understand information presented in a variety of genres on familiar topics, even when something unexpected is expressed.	I can understand the main idea and some supporting details on a variety of topics of personal and general interest. I can follow stories and descriptions of some length and in various time frames and genres.

Table 38. NCSSFL-ACTFL Global Can-Do Benchmarks (continued)

Level/Mode	Interpersonal Communication	Presentational Speaking	Presentational Writing	Interpretive Listening	Interpretive Reading
Advanced Mid	I can express myself fully not only on familiar topics but also on some concrete social, academic, and professional topics. I can talk in detail and in an organized way about events and experiences in various time frames. I can confidently handle routine situations with an unexpected complication. I can share my point of view in discussions on some complex issues.	I can deliver well-organized presentations on concrete social, academic, and professional topics. I can present detailed information about events and experiences in various time frames.	I can write on a wide variety of general interest, professional, and academic topics. I can write well-organized, detailed paragraphs in various time frames.	I can understand the main idea and most supporting details on a variety of topics of personal and general interest, as well as some topics of professional interest. I can follow stories and descriptions of some length and in various time frames. I can understand information presented in most genres, even when not familiar with the topic.	I can understand the main idea and most supporting details in texts on a variety of topics of personal and general interest, as well as some professional topics. I can follow stories and descriptions of considerable length and in various time frames. I can understand texts written in a variety of genres, even when I am unfamiliar with the topic.
Advanced High	I can express myself freely and spontaneously, and for the most part accurately, on concrete topics and on most complex issues. I can usually support my opinion and develop hypotheses on topics of particular interest or personal expertise.	I can deliver detailed presentations, usually with accuracy, clarity, and precision, on a variety of topics and issues related to community interests and some special fields of expertise.	I can write extensively with significant precision and detail on a variety of topics, most complex issues, and some special fields of expertise.	I can easily follow narrative, informational, and descriptive speech. I can understand discussions on most topics that deal with special interests, unfamiliar situations, and abstract concepts. I can sometimes follow extended arguments and different points of view.	I can easily follow narrative, informational, and descriptive texts. I can understand what I read on most topics that deal with special interests, unfamiliar situations, and abstract concepts. I can sometimes understand extended arguments and different points of view.
Superior	I can communicate with ease, accuracy, and fluency. I can participate fully and effectively in discussions on a variety of topics in formal and informal settings. I can discuss at length complex issues by structuring arguments and developing hypotheses.	I can deliver detailed presentations with accuracy, clarity, and precision to a wide variety of audiences on topics and issues ranging from broad general interests to areas of specialized expertise.	I can write about complex and abstract issues ranging from topics of broad general interests to areas of specialized expertise using standard structure, lexicon, and writing protocols.	I can follow a wide range of academic and professional discourse on abstract and specialized topics. I can understand all standard dialects. I can sometimes infer complex meaning that requires deep understanding of the culture.	I can follow academic, professional, and literary texts on a wide range of both familiar and unfamiliar subjects. I can sometimes infer complex meaning that requires analysis and deep understanding of the culture.
Distinguished	I can communicate reflectively on a wide range of global issues and highly abstract concepts in a culturally sophisticated manner.	I can deliver sophisticated and articulate presentations on a wide range of global issues and highly abstract concepts in a culturally appropriate manner, tailored to a variety of audiences.	I can write about global issues from highly conceptualized and analytical perspectives. I can tailor my writing to sophisticated readers.	I can understand highly abstract and specialized speech tailored to different audiences. I can understand sophisticated language, humor, and persuasive arguments embedded with cultural references and allusions.	I can understand with ease and confidence highly abstract and specialized texts that are succinct or elaborate. I can follow unpredictable turns of thought. I can manage inference from within the cultural framework.

Performance Descriptors. With the pathway toward proficiency in mind, classroom teachers can turn to the ACTFL Performance Descriptors for Language Learners (ACTFL, 2012b) for guidance in designing appropriate assessments for their learners. Performance is described for three modes of communication in Novice, Intermediate, and Advanced ranges according to seven language domains. Three of the domains describe the parameters for the learner's performance: Functions, Contexts and Content, Text Type (Table 39).

Table 39. ACTFL Performance Descriptors Language Domains: Parameters of Performance

Domain	Parameters of Performance	Examples
Functions	What types of communication can the learner understand and use (global tasks)?	Ask and answer questions Describe a person, place, thing Express likes, dislikes with reasons Tell a story with detailed descriptions
Contexts and Content	What are the contexts (situations) in which the learner can communicate? What are the topics that the learner can understand and discuss?	Oneself Family Community Interests Professions Global issues
Text Type	What types of texts can the learner understand and produce in order to be a novice, intermediate, or advanced communicator?	Words Phrases Sentences Questions Strings of sentences Paragraphs

The four remaining domains—Language Control, Vocabulary, Communication Strategies, Cultural Awareness—describe how and how well the learner understands and can be understood (Table 40).

Table 40. ACTFL Performance Descriptors Language Domains: Qualities of Performance

Domain	Qualities of performance	What it describes
Language Control	How accurate is the language?	Learner's level of control over the language he/she uses
Vocabulary	How broad is the vocabulary?	The number of topics and related specificity that a learner can address
Communication Strategies	How does the learner maintain communication?	Strategies to negotiate meaning and express oneself
Cultural Awareness	How is cultural knowledge reflected in language use?	Products, practices, and perspectives used to communicate successfully

The ACTFL Performance Descriptors for Language Learners are located in Appendix E. ACTFL notes that the descriptions are intentionally broad so that they can be adapted to language learners of all ages (ACTFL, 2012b). We will reference the Performance Descriptors are referenced in discussing assessment of and for learning in the next section.

Formative and Summative Assessments

Assessments can be broadly divided into two categories: *formative* and *summative*. Formative assessments, introduced in Chapter 2, are assessments *for* learning and take place throughout the daily lessons of a unit providing helpful feedback to both teacher and learners. This feedback tells learners how well they know and understand the content of the lesson. Teachers use this feedback to make adjustments to lesson plans and pacing as appropriate: slowing down to allow more practice; reteaching using different types of explanations, examples, and learning activities when learners have not grasped a concept; or moving forward more quickly when learners demonstrate that they are comfortable with the new concepts. Formative assessments provide valuable insights about individual learners' strengths and challenges in meeting the goals and objectives of a lesson or class, opening the way for differentiation of instruction to meet the needs of all learners. (See Chapter 3 for more information on differentiation.) Since formative assessments are assessments for learning and not final measures of specific unit goals, they do not have to be graded. They are practice sessions similar to orchestra or choir rehearsals, or scrimmages in a sport, intended to give feedback to the learners on how well they know and can use the language, and where more practice is needed. Keeping a record of the formative assessments is helpful in showing learners the relationship between practice and final performance, but it is the final summative performance assessment that shows what learners know and can do related to the unit goals and objectives.

Summative assessments, assessments *of* learning, evaluate learning at the conclusion of a defined instructional period such as the end of a unit, semester, course, or program. They are designed to indicate whether and to what degree the learners have met the goals of instruction. In language classrooms, summative assessments should be performance-based and evaluate how well the learners can communicate in the three modes of communication: interpersonal, interpretive, and presentational. In this publication, the performance assessment is written at the beginning of the unit template, immediately following the essential question and unit goals. This placement models the philosophy of Understanding by Design (Wiggins & McTighe, 2005): beginning with the end in mind. Summative assessments should capture the most important learning of the unit and provide a venue for learners to apply that learning to real-life situations.

Formative Assessments: Techniques for Monitoring Learner Progress. There are many ways to monitor learner progress during lessons. The teacher may choose to track performance during various activities. Learners may monitor their peers and provide feedback, or learners may self-assess or reflect at different points during the lesson. A learner-centered classroom requires that learners take increased responsibility for their own learning and evaluate their individual progress toward goals and objectives.

Learner Can-Do: Since goals were shared with learners at the beginning of the unit, learners should take time to reflect on their progress toward the goals. A portion of a student self-assessment template appears in Table 41. NCSSFL-ACTFL Global Can-Do Benchmarks may be used to create the generic goal, but unit-specific Can-Do Statements allow learners to reflect on progress toward specific unit goals and develop a sense of self-empowerment towards their own learning. Older learners can track progress on the template. Have learners add a check or date to indicate where they are in terms of meeting a goal and then allow time for them to re-evaluate progress throughout the unit. They may reflect individually or may be asked to prove to a peer that they can meet a goal. Learners should also be challenged to reflect on how they might provide evidence for these statements, and may be expected to post evidence in electronic

portfolios. In class, learners may simply work with a partner to "prove" that they can meet the individual goals. Younger learners may have images to color or may be given stickers to place on a chart as they accomplish key goals.

Table 41. Learner Can-Do Chart

I can:	Yes	With help	This is still a goal
discuss my lifestyle routine and find out about how others spend their time			
discuss health/lifestyle balance issues and needs with others			
respond to and offer suggestions on how to create a balanced lifestyle			

Homework Checks. Quick homework checks will also allow learners to assess their understanding of a concept. The teacher may opt to circulate throughout the classroom assessing for completion while noticing one or two particular answers to ensure that learners have been thoughtful when completing the work. Use a homework chart noting a + (plus) for complete and reasonably accurate, a ✓ (check) for mostly complete, fairly accurate or a – (minus) for incomplete or mostly inaccurate. As the teacher circulates, learners check their answers against the posted answers and are encouraged to ask questions of the teacher or classmates if they do not understand. The responsibility for learning is shifted to the learner.

Fluency Counts: Fluency counts are another way to allow learners to self-assess. Pick a topic and ask learners to write on that topic for a specific amount of time. Tell them not to worry too much about accuracy, the goal is to get their ideas on paper. When time is called, have learners count the number of words they wrote about the topic. Do this frequently so that learners can see that they are writing more in the same amount of time. If learners get stuck, encourage them to write the same word over and over until they think of something else to write. A similar fluency count can be used for speaking tasks. Pair learners. Have one learner do a monologue for a certain amount of time. Have the other learner count the number of words or sentences that are said. When time is called have the listener give the count, but also give suggestions on what else might have been said. Learners should see the quantity of speech increasing over time (Tuttle & Tuttle, 2012). To move from presentational speaking to interpersonal speaking, pair learners for spontaneous conversations. Create the context for a meaningful conversation and challenge learners to engage in conversation for a specific amount of time. Tell them to start over if they run out of things to say or to redo the conversation with a change in the order of their ideas. Doing this type of conversation practice frequently allows learners to see that it is getting easier to sustain a meaningful conversation for longer and longer periods of time. It may seem contrived to time the conversations of the learners, but language learning is a skill and many skills are assessed with timers. The runner who runs a 100-meter race is delighted to take a second off his time. Language learners feel a similar success as they increase their performance within a specific time frame.

Teacher Can-Do: With large classes, multiple sections, and a variety of preps during a regular teaching day, teachers may find it helpful to document learner performance toward goals throughout the unit. Knowing more precisely where individual learners are in the learning process allows for more informed feedback. Teachers can create an adapted version of the Learner Can-Do Chart described earlier. Run the unit goals across the top of the chart and the learner names down the left column. Table 42 is an example of the Teacher Can-Do Chart. As learners work in class, place a check when you hear or see that a learner has demonstrated meeting a goal. The advantage of such a system is that it serves as a continual reminder throughout the unit of who may need additional help or of which goals may need to be reintroduced.

Table 42. Teacher Can-Do Chart

	I can discuss my lifestyle routine and find out about how others spend their time	I can discuss health/ lifestyle balance issues and needs with others	I can respond to and offer suggestions on how to create a balanced lifestyle
Student 1			
Student 2			
Student 3			

T.A.L.K. Scores. During pair or group work, circulate and monitor individual learners for staying in the target (T) language, for their accuracy (A) on specific structures, for their ability to listen (L) and respond appropriately and for their ability to be kind (K) by being an equal conversational partner in an activity (T.A.L.K.). T.A.L.K. scores allow teachers to track learner performance during various speaking activities. Create a chart (Table 43) that has a column for each domain across the top and the name of each learner on the vertical column. Use a

system to indicate performance such as + Consistently, ✓ Few difficulties, – Many difficulties (Shrum & Glisan, 2010).

Table 43. T.A.L.K. Scores

	Target Language	Accuracy	Listen	Kind
Student A	+	–	✓	✓
Student B	+	✓	+	–
Student C				

Index Cards: Create an index card for each learner (Table 44). Allow learners to pair using a strategy such as think–pair–share. Then, call on three or four non-volunteering learners to give the answer. Learners who have practiced with their partner or group should be able to give a solid answer. A good answer scores a 10. A zero is given only when learners do not know what they are supposed to do, and have obviously not used the practice time to develop answers. Use the index cards over the course of a marking period to increase individual accountability during pair and group work.

Table 44. Index Card

Student Name						
Question #1	10	9	8	7	6	0
Question#2	10	9	8	7	6	0
Question #3	10	9	8	7	6	0

Exit Slips. The sample lesson used an exit slip near the end of the class. Exit slips work well when the teacher would like to see in writing how well an individual learner is able to meet the lesson objective. In this case, the learners were asked to write words and phrases that explained an expression introduced in class. Direct the learners to write as much as they can for a specific amount of time. Collect the exit slips as learners leave. Exit slips are formative assessment (i.e., assessment for learning) and there is no need to grade this work. Instead, simply review the exit slips and pull out the ones for learners who did not make sufficient progress toward the lesson objective. Keep those slips as a reminder to provide additional support to those learners during the next lesson.

Summative Assessments: Rubrics and Scoring Guides. Evaluating performance on summative tasks requires careful thought. As teachers design the performance assessment tasks for a unit, they should concurrently determine the characteristics of high-quality performance. Based on those characteristics, the teacher creates rubrics to provide the learner with clear criteria by which the performance will be evaluated. Those rubrics then provide feedback on the strengths of the performance and suggestions for continuous improvement. Tedick (2002) states that rubrics also:

- help learners set goals and take responsibility for their learning by clarifying expectations for performance;
- help learners develop their ability to self-assess their own work in terms of quality;
- help others (parents, administrators, colleagues) understand the criteria for excellent performance;
- increase an assessment's reliability through well-defined criteria that can be applied consistently across individual performances; and
- align criteria to standards, curriculum, and performance descriptors.

As noted in Tedick's final point, rubrics align criteria to standards, curriculum, and *performance* descriptors. ACTFL's Performance Descriptors for Language Learners (ACTFL, 2012b) "identify appropriate learning targets for language learners who begin at any age or grade level (pre-kindergarten, elementary school, middle school, high school, or postsecondary institutions) and whose language learning continues for varying amounts of time" (p. 3). ACTFL provides an important note in the 2012 edition of the Performance Descriptors:

> The *Performance Descriptors* form a roadmap for teaching and learning, helping teachers create performance tasks targeted to the appropriate range, while challenging learners to also use strategies from the next higher range. In an instructional environment, the content and tasks are controlled, resulting in higher expectations of learners' performance compared to how they perform in a non-instructional environment. For example, Novice language learners use highly practiced and memorized sentences and questions within the supportive learning environment and within known contexts even though they are not yet Intermediate-level language users (p. 3).

The Performance Descriptors are helpful to classroom teachers as they determine the performance tasks for a unit of instruction. A teacher might think while planning the assessment: "This task is for my second year learners. I know that they are still functioning as Novices, but for this particular interview task, I am going to ask them to include a variety of questions for the interview that they create. This will be a good way to

nudge them beyond asking the memorized questions we have practiced since the beginning of the year. Because we are working on questions in class, I know that they have the scaffolding needed to create a variety of questions for the interview. My students are still Novice learners but they are starting to practice some of the skills (understanding, asking, and answering a variety of questions) they will need in order to be considered an Intermediate learner. I referred to the Performance Descriptors to help me think about where my learners are now and what the next step is to increase their proficiency." This teacher would be able to design the rubric based on the background knowledge of what performance looks like at the Novice, Intermediate, and Advanced levels, and the notes she had written about the criteria as she was designing the unit's summative performance tasks.

You will see in the examples that a three-tiered rubric is recommended with headers of "Strong Performance," "Meets Expectations," and "Approaching Expectations." With a three-tiered rubric, all three levels should describe varying degrees of success in completing the task. In a four-tiered rubric, the fourth column is labeled "Does Not Meet Expectations" and generally includes descriptors that indicate that the requirements for the product or performance were not met. This advocacy for the three-tiered rubric is based on the belief that when units are constructed according to the guidelines in this publication, teachers will provide the scaffolding that learners need in order to demonstrate the unit goals. Later in this section is a discussion about using a checklist of "non-negotiables" to help learners self-assess, making sure that they have met the requirements for the product or performance. Learners can achieve one of the described levels of performance in a three-tiered rubric if they pay attention to the criteria by which they will be evaluated, actively participate in all the learning activities in and outside of class leading up to the summative assessment, and act on the feedback suggestions given on formative assessments. A performance that is below "Approaching Expectations" requires sending the learner "back to the drawing board" to work on improving the performance.

Notice that the headers describing levels of performance are not "Novice," "Intermediate," and "Advanced." The rubrics are designed to give feedback to the learners on a specific performance with specific criteria. Therefore, it is more appropriate to describe the product or performance as "Strong," "Meets Expectations," or "Approaching Expectations." While

Table 45. Rubric for the Balanced Lifestyle Interpersonal Task

	Strong Performance 10 9	Meets Expectations 8	Approaching Expectations 7
How well am I understood? (Domain: Language Control)	I am easily understood. Errors in speaking are minor and do not interfere with communication.	I am understood most of the time. I may need to repeat or reword occasionally. Errors in speaking do not interfere with communication.	I am difficult to understand at times I may ask for help expressing ideas (e.g., "How do you say . . . ?"). Some errors in speaking may interfere with communication.
How involved am I in the conversation? (Domains: Functions, Text Type)	I ask a variety of relevant questions to keep the conversation going. I can respond to questions and/or add follow-up comments/ information. I encourage others to participate.	I ask relevant questions to keep the conversation going. I can respond to questions and/or make a follow-up comment.	I ask a few relevant questions; I respond to questions simply.
What communication strategies do I use? (Domain: Communication Strategies)	I ask for clarification as needed. If I don't know a word, I can explain it another way (circumlocution).	I ask for repetition as needed. If I don't know a word, I can use gestures and drawings to express what I mean.	I can say "I don't understand" as needed. If I don't know a word, I quit talking.
How do I demonstrate that I can correctly use the new vocabulary from the unit? (Domains: Vocabulary, Contexts/ Content)	I successfully use many new words related to the unit to discuss the assigned topic.	I successfully use a few new words related to the unit to discuss the assigned topic.	I successfully use familiar words related to the unit to discuss the assigned topic.
What cultural knowledge and understandings do I share? (Domain: Cultural Awareness)	I add relevant information about the target culture. I use cultural gestures and/or expressions that imitate those that a native speaker would use.	I refer to relevant information about the target culture. I may imitate some cultural gestures and/or expressions that a native speaker would use.	I make limited or no references to the target culture. I may use a cultural gesture or expression that I have learned in class.

the rubric is informed by the characteristics of Novice, Intermediate, or Advanced, the rubric needs to be task-specific in order to provide focused feedback for improvement.

Rubrics for the Performance Assessment Tasks in the Balanced Lifestyle Unit. Table 45 is a rubric for the interpersonal mode used to evaluate performance in the model unit about a balanced lifestyle. The final interpersonal performance task states:

In pairs or small groups, learners share what they have learned about their lifestyle and the lifestyle of teenagers in France in terms of a balanced lifestyle. They compare their daily routines and schedules and make and respond to suggestions to adjust their lifestyle.

Notice these features of this rubric:

- The criteria used to evaluate performance are presented in the form of questions. This allows the learners to self-assess their performance; the questions are free of jargon, making them easy to understand. The appropriate domains of the Performance Descriptors are listed after each question. The actual names of the domains are not intended to be used in rubrics for learners.

- There are five questions to evaluate performance which is a manageable number for both the learner and the teacher to keep in mind during the performance.

- The question associated with the domain of cultural awareness asks: "What cultural knowledge and understandings do I share?" The descriptors of performance address both knowledge and behaviors.

- This rubric is a three-tier rubric with the ratings of "Strong Performance," "Meets Expectations," and "Approaching Expectations." The "Strong Performance" appears first if you read left to right. This sets the stage for the learners, describing excellence in interpersonal communication. This rubric does not include a fourth rating of "Not Meeting Expectations." Instead, the rubric describes performances that reflect acceptable degrees of competence, placing all learners on the pathway towards proficiency.

- The three tiers of the rubric have numbers for scoring the performance: 10 or 9 = strong performance; 8 = meets expectations; 7 = approaching expectations. The rating for each category can be added together to arrive at a score that can be transferred to a grade book.

- The descriptors in this rubric can be applied to Novice- and Intermediate-level language learners. In interpersonal communication, the characteristics of successful performance remain the same. However, the topic that learners discuss becomes more detailed and complex.

- The descriptors for "How well am I understood?" allow for minor errors that do not interfere with communication. It is important for learners to understand that the emphasis is on comprehensibility, not perfection.

Table 47 is the rubric for the presentational task about a balanced lifestyle. The descriptor of the task is:

Learners will create a presentation that can be shared via the Internet based on multiple sources of information highlighting ways to promote a balanced lifestyle for teenagers. The presentation will be shared with another French class.

The descriptor for this presentational task allows learners to determine the types of media they will use to create the product. Their parameters are that the information must be based on multiple sources, the topic must be about ways to promote balanced lifestyles for teenagers, and the product must be able to be shared via the Internet.

Presentational tasks require rough drafts or rehearsals with coaching and/or feedback to improve the final product because the final products will be shared with an audience beyond the classroom. The guidelines for the final product are "non-negotiables" designed to outline the minimum requirements of content for the product. Here is a potential list of non-negotiables for the task about a balanced lifestyle:

- Work collaboratively with one or two other people;
- Create a bibliography documenting the sources for the presentation:
  - Sources discussed in class should be included as appropriate
  - Three authentic French sources not discussed in class must be included
  - May include up to three authentic American sources
- Incorporate written and spoken text in the final product;
- Include at least three ways to promote a balanced lifestyle;
- Include references to balanced lifestyles of French teenagers; and
- Upload final product to class webpage.

The checklist of non-negotiables helps learners verify that they have followed directions and included the components needed for evaluation. A product that does not conform to these guidelines should not be evaluated because the product is incomplete. The requirement to meet all the non-negotiables

before submitting the product for evaluation allows the evaluation to focus on the quality of the final product as described in the rubric.

When preparing a presentational task, learners benefit from following the Five-Step Writing Process in Table 46. This process is applicable to any written or oral presentational task. Notice that feedback is given throughout the process by peers and the teacher so that the final product is polished, ready for publication or performance.

Table 46. Five-Step Writing Process

Five-Step Writing Process
Step 1: Brainstorming
• Brainstorm ideas about the topic • Look for information from among the reading, listening, and viewing tasks completed during the unit • Research further information online • Create a bibliography listing all the sources you consulted
Step 2: Drafting
• Create categories related to the topic • Organize the information into topics • Look for similarities and differences in the information • Determine a key message for your presentation • Create an outline of ideas you plan to use in your presentation • Determine the type of media you will use to deliver your presentation • Write a script for your presentation • Exchange your script with another group in order to give feedback to each other about the content
Step 3: Revising
• Discuss the feedback received from another group • Make changes to your script as appropriate • Look up unknown words in a dictionary • Read your script aloud to your group to see if it makes sense • Submit your script to your teacher for comment
Step 4: Final editing
• Review the comments from your teacher • Make corrections to the script; clarify any comments from the teacher that you do not understand • Have your peer review group read the corrected version and make comments • For oral presentations, practice the script out loud; for written presentations, create the final product
Step 5: Publishing/Broadcasting
• Share the finished product

Table 47 is a rubric to evaluate the balanced lifestyle presentational task.

Table 47. Rubric for the Balanced Lifestyle Presentational Task

	Strong Performance 10 9	Meets Expectations 8	Approaching Expectations 7
Are we understood? (Domain: Language Control)	Pronunciation imitates a French accent. Any errors in pronunciation do not interfere with understanding. Speech is smooth and natural with few hesitations.	Accent generally imitates a French accent. Errors in pronunciation rarely interfere with understanding. Speech sounds like a script is being read at times, and/or may be delivered too quickly.	Accent sounds more American than French. Errors in pronunciation may occasionally interfere with understanding. Speech sounds like a script is being read and delivery lacks natural intonation.
How are tech tools used in my presentation? (Domain: Communication Strategies)	Visuals and sound and design are used effectively to emphasize the key ideas in the presentation, to help the audience follow the storyline of the presentation, and to maintain the audience's attention.	Visuals and/or sound and design in the presentation help the audience focus on the key ideas and follow the sequence of information.	Visuals and/or sound and design are used in the presentation. Key ideas are sometimes difficult to identify because at times there may be too many visuals or sound/design elements.
Is the presentation interesting and informative? (Domains: Functions, Contexts/Content)	The content of the presentation is thoughtfully selected with the audience and purpose in mind. The information is accurate and the recommendations for balance provide useful tips and tools for teenagers.	The content of the presentation is selected with the audience and purpose in mind. The information is accurate and the recommendations for balance are appropriate for teenagers.	The content of the presentation is selected according to instructions but needs more careful thought in terms of what information is interesting and informative for an audience of teenagers. The information is accurate.
How rich is the vocabulary? (Domain: Vocabulary)	Wide variety of familiar vocabulary is used correctly and appropriately, incorporating many new expressions from the current unit of study,	Variety of familiar vocabulary is used correctly and appropriately, incorporating several new expressions from the current unit of study.	Simple, familiar vocabulary is used correctly, incorporating a few new expressions from the current unit of study.
How are knowledge and understanding of the target culture represented? (Domain: Cultural Awareness)	Information about the target culture is accurately presented; the relationships among products, practices, and perspectives are included and justified within the presentation.	Information about the target culture is accurately presented; products, practices, and perspectives are identified and some relationships are included within the presentation.	Information about the target culture is presented; products, practices, and perspectives are identified.

Notice that this rubric is designed to evaluate a product that has been produced by a group where all group members receive the same grade. It is a three-tier rubric; the criteria to evaluate performance are presented as five questions with the associated domains listed after each question. The descriptors reflect qualities of a multimedia presentation. Cultural understanding is evaluated based on the explanation of how a cultural product is connected to a cultural practice, and how they both work together to provide insights into the target culture (perspectives). Because of the five-step writing process (Table 46) with feedback on the drafts of the script for the final presentation, the language in the final presentation should be accurate and is, therefore, not addressed as a separate item in the rubric. The intent is to create a product that is ready for publication. The descriptors in this rubric can be applied to Novice, Intermediate, and Advanced learners.

Note about the presentational mode: Performance or products generated in the presentational mode are meant to be polished, benefiting from multiple drafts and rehearsals with ongoing feedback because the final performances or products are shared with an audience beyond the classroom. Learners work to showcase their very best writing or speaking. However, there are times when a teacher may want to gather evidence of how well learners write without the benefit of drafts and feedback. This is often referred to as "on-demand" writing. At beginning proficiency levels, learners may write a few simple sentences; at more advanced levels, they may be expected to write one or more paragraphs on a topic. Teachers may assign a topic that addresses some or all of the unit goals and may opt to have learners write in class to ensure that they are capable of writing the piece without outside support. Learners would have a limited amount of time to draft and revise without receiving any external feedback, and the teacher would score the assignment knowing that the learner had written without the benefit of that feedback. For the balanced lifestyle unit, learners might be asked to write on demand to describe their lives in terms of balance and would be required to complete the writing assignment in class. The instructions might be:

> Consider your lifestyle in terms of balance. Explain what you do and don't do. Compare your actions to French teenagers, drawing on information from the texts we have used in class. End by setting a personal goal and explain why this goal is appropriate for you.

The rubric for on-demand writing would be similar in structure to the one used for presentational writing, but the questions and domains would change slightly to reflect the fact that learners wrote this on their own without additional support. Table 48 shows a rubric for on-demand writing.

The interpretive mode is also assessed in a Standards-based performance assessment. For this unit on a balanced lifestyle, the assessment includes three authentic texts: (1) reading a blog written by a teenager; (2) watching a commercial; and (3) reading the daily schedule of a top athlete. These authentic texts provide information that learners can use to complete the presentational task. They also give additional information that learners can reference in the interpersonal task.

The interpretive tasks do not have to be completed at the end of the unit. The teacher can give one of the texts as a summative assessment at a point in time during the unit when the learners have sufficient vocabulary and strategies to interpret that text independently.

For the interpretive tasks, we are using scoring guides to evaluate performance. Since the focus is on comprehension of the texts, teachers may ask that learners use some English to demonstrate comprehension especially for beginning language learners with limited vocabulary. Shrum and Glisan (2010) note that several research studies show that learners demonstrate greater comprehension of a text when they can use their native language to explain what they understood. Shrum and Glisan recommend that teachers consider the proficiency levels of the learners and the task they are asked to accomplish in determining the need for learners to use English in interpretive tasks.

For the blog about what a French teenager does daily, learners demonstrate understanding by checking off the activities that the teenager does from a list of possible activities. The responses are either correct or incorrect. Next, the learner evaluates the balance in the French teenager's life based on the activities that the teenager does, and compares them to his/her own and what he/she has learned about lifestyles of French teenagers in general. The evaluation is a simple scoring guide with space for comments about the responses. Table 49 shows the scoring guide for this task.

Table 48. Rubric for On-Demand Writing

	Strong Performance 10 9	Meets Expectations 8	Approaching Expectations 7
Am I understood? (Domain: Language Control)	My writing is clearly understood; the reader understands the writer's intent without extra effort. Errors do not interfere with message.	My writing is generally understood; but reader may have to occasionally reread a phrase or sentence to understand. Errors do not interfere with message.	My writing is generally understood, but the reader may have to be willing to make a guess or reread to understand. Errors occur and do cause some confusion for the reader.
How rich is my vocabulary? (Domain: Vocabulary)	I use a wide variety of familiar vocabulary correctly and appropriately. I incorporate new expressions from the current unit of study.	I use a variety of familiar vocabulary, correctly and appropriately. I incorporate a few new expressions from the current unit of study.	I use simple, familiar vocabulary, correctly. I may use a few new expressions from the current unit of study.
How well do I complete the task? (Domain: Functions, Content and Context)	I complete each part of the task adding some details.	I complete each part of the task.	I complete most of the task.
How organized is my writing? (Domain: Text Type)	My ideas are presented in an organized manner. My sentences are varied and interesting and I use transitions to connect my thoughts.	My ideas are presented in a somewhat logical manner. I have some interesting sentences and use transitions to connect my thoughts.	My ideas are shared in a random fashion. My sentences follow a predictable pattern.
How are knowledge and understanding of the target culture represented? (Domain: Cultural Awareness)	Comparisons between French and American culture are accurately presented.	Information about the target culture is accurately presented.	Information about the target culture is presented, but may or may not be accurate.

Table 49. Scoring Guide for Interpretive Task: Balanced Lifestyle Blog

	Yes	Partially	No
1. Your evaluation of the degree to which the French teenager leads a balanced lifestyle is based on evidence from the blog and is logical.			
2. You compare the French teenager's schedule to your own, indicating similarities and differences.			
3. You conclude with observations about the degree to which the French teenager's lifestyle reflects what you learned in this unit about lifestyles of French teenagers.			
Comments:			

The second interpretive task states: Learners will watch a commercial for a product that promises to make life easier or less stressful, and will demonstrate comprehension by analyzing the effectiveness of the message and product. For this task, the learner is demonstrating comprehension of the language through the analysis of the commercial. Based on two criteria that advertising agencies consider in designing effective commercials, learners respond to questions that check understanding of the language while also analyzing the quality of the commercial. A final question asks learners to make cultural comparisons. Learners respond to these prompts:

1. The visual matches the product.
   a. What is the name of the product?
   b. What is the product used for?
   c. Does the visual match the product? Why or why not?
2. The message is honest.
   a. What does the commercial say that the product will do?
   b. Is the claim an honest assessment of the product? Why or why not?
3. The product is made and sold in France.
   a. Do you think that this product is popular in France? Why or why not?
   b. Do you think this product would be popular in the United States? Why or why not?

The scoring guide below evaluates the learner's responses. The teacher indicates if the response is accurate/logical and complete. Note that the teacher will need to explain and give examples of the qualities of "accurate," "logical," and "complete" responses before the learners complete the task. Table 50 shows the scoring guide for this task.

The third interpretive task asks learners to read a schedule of a top athlete to determine how he spends the hours in his day, deciding what elements are part of a balanced lifestyle and what elements are missing. Learners check off the items on the athlete's schedule that contribute to a balanced lifestyle. Next the learners list the elements of balance that are missing. Finally the learners explain why the checked items on the schedule contribute to a balanced lifestyle and how the missing

Table 50. Scoring Guide for Balanced Lifestyle Interpretive Task: Commercial

	The response is accurate/logical.			The response is complete.		
	Yes	Partially	No	Yes	Partially	No
1a. What is the name of the product?						
1b. What is the product used for?						
1c. Does the visual match the product? Why or why not?						
2a. What does the commercial say that the product will do?						
2b. Is the claim an honest assessment of the product? Why or why not?						
3a. Do you think that this product is popular in France? Why or why not?						
3b. Do you think this product would be popular in the United States? Why or why not?						
Comments:						

items would improve his/her balance in life. Table 51 shows the scoring guide for this task.

Table 51. Scoring Guide to Evaluate Athlete's Daily Schedule.

	Yes	Partially	No
1. You accurately identified the portions of the athlete's schedule that contribute to a balanced lifestyle.			
2. You accurately identified the elements that are missing from a balanced lifestyle.			
3. The explanation you wrote about balance in the athlete's lifestyle is based on evidence from his schedule and what you have learned about a balanced lifestyle.			
Comments:			

Growth in Interculturality

Summary: Evaluating Summative Performance Assessment Tasks. All together, the rubrics and scoring guides for the three modes of communication give a complete picture of how well the learners can understand and use the target language on the topic of a balanced lifestyle. In terms of culture, notice that cultural awareness is a separate category in the rubrics for the interpersonal and presentational tasks. For the interpretive mode, in two of the three tasks, the learners need to make cultural comparisons as part of the comprehension questions for the texts.

Documenting growth in interculturality. As learners increase their abilities to understand and communicate in a language other than English, they are also building cultural understanding or interculturality. The Council of Europe (2008) describes the connection between language learning and culture: "Language learning helps learners to avoid stereotyping individuals, to develop curiosity and openness to others, and to discover other cultures. Language learning helps learners to see that interaction with individuals having different social identities and cultures is an enriching experience" (p. 29).

Byram (1997) describes cultural competence in terms of five *savoirs*:

- *Savoirs:* Knowledge of social groups and their related products and practices within one's own country and within the country of the person with whom you are communicating; knowledge of historical and contemporary relationships among countries;

- *Savoir être:* Curiosity and openness, readiness to suspend disbelief about other cultures and belief about one's own;
- *Savoir comprendre:* Ability to interpret a document or event from another culture, explain it and relate it to documents and events from one's own culture;
- *Savoir apprendre/faire:* Ability to acquire new knowledge of a culture and cultural practices, and ability to use this knowledge to interact with people from other cultures in real time; and
- *Savoir s'engager:* Ability to evaluate, critically and on the basis of explicit criteria, products, practices, and perspectives in one's own and in other cultures and countries.

Taken collectively the five *savoirs* capture what it means to have a deep or enduring understanding of culture. Learners truly understand when they demonstrate their ability in each of the six facets of understanding: explanation, interpretation, application, perspective, empathy, and self-knowledge. A learner who truly understands can explain, interpret, apply, empathize, and can demonstrate that they have perspective and self-knowledge (Wiggins & McTighe, 1998).

The *Standards for Language Learning in the 21st Century Revised 3rd Edition* (NSFLEP, 2006) summarizes the purpose for learning languages as represented through the 5 Cs of Communication, Cultures, Connections, Comparisons, and Communities: "Knowing how, when, and why to say what to whom" (p. 11), making it clear that it takes both language and culture for successful communication.

Jacobson, Sleicher, and Burke (1999) compare learning to communicate in a new culture to learning a new type of art, recommending that the best way to show what you have learned is by giving examples from your experiences. Documenting and reflecting on experiences with the other cultures is how the European Language Portfolio and LinguaFolio address growth in interculturality.

Schulz (2007) suggests that learners keep a portfolio that documents their interactions with other cultures and their reflections on those interactions:

> Just as second language acquisition is not a uniform, instantaneous event but occurs in a spiral fashion over time, necessitating repeated language input and output opportunities, the development of cultural awareness and cross-cultural understanding also occurs over time in cyclical fashion, permitting learners to document their emerging awareness and understanding with new data and insights (p. 9).

Schulz identifies the following objectives for a cultural portfolio, and gives suggestions for ways to meet each objective:

1. Students develop and demonstrate an awareness that geographic, historical, economic, social/religious, and political factors can have an impact on cultural products, practices, and perspectives, including language use and styles of communication.
   - Suggested task: Compare the United States and target country in at least 10 ways. Use the information researched to discuss at least five similarities/differences and how they influence the culture.
   - Suggested task: Identify at least five culture products and explain why the products are popular in the target country.

2. Students develop and demonstrate an awareness that situational variables such as age, gender, religion, place of residence, and time shape interactions and behaviors among people in important ways.
   - Suggested task: Comment on a minimum of three examples of observed differences in native or first language (L1) usage by, for example, younger and older persons, male and female speakers, southern and northern speakers.
   - Suggested task: Examine authentic texts from the second or target language (L2) culture to find examples of how people address each other.
   - Suggested task: Describe and comment on a minimum of three behaviors that illustrate similarities and differences between the target culture and your own.

3. Students recognize stereotypes or generalizations about the home and target cultures and evaluate them in terms of supporting evidence.
   - Suggested task: Give three examples of stereotypes of Americans and discuss how these might have developed.
   - Suggested task: Give three examples of stereotypes of people from the target culture and discuss how these might have developed.
   - Suggested task: Conduct a survey of friends, family, and community members to explore stereotypes they might hold about the people from the target culture.

4. Students develop and demonstrate an awareness that each language and culture has culture-conditioned images and culture-specific connotations of some words, phrases, proverbs, idiomatic expressions, gestures, and symbols.
   - Suggested task: List and explain culture-specific connotations in words or phrases you have encountered in L2.

5. Students develop and demonstrate an awareness of some types of causes of cultural misunderstanding between members of different cultures.
   - Suggested task: using newspaper articles, advertisements, or websites, compare how an event, product, or practice of the home culture is viewed in the target culture and attempt to explain the reasons for the views.

This chapter provided multiple examples of formative and summative tools for assessing growth in both linguistic skills and cultural understanding. The importance of developing learners' ability to self-assess their progress in both these areas was highlighted through the use of LinguaFolio or a similar portfolio. In all cases, it is important that growth in cultural understanding be addressed intentionally just like growth in language skills. Rubrics and scoring guides must include culture in the criteria for evaluating a performance. Learners must have opportunities to reflect on their encounters with other cultures over time and the amount of growth in their communication skills. In the concluding chapter, we describe the mindset for curriculum development.

Application

1. You are working with a group of colleagues to design a rubric for interpersonal tasks. A colleague wants to use proficiency levels as the levels in the rubric. What would you say and how would you explain your rationale? What would you suggest as an alternative?

2. You are working with a colleague to design an interpretive assessment at the Novice level. Your colleague wants to write all of the comprehension questions in the target language. You believe strongly that English should be used. What would you say to justify your point of view?

3. You are working with a new colleague who has very large classes. She is struggling to implement formative assessment as a part of her lessons. What would you suggest?

Reflection

1. How does my gradebook reflect performance in the three modes of communication? To what extent is the learner's grade reflective of what they can do with the language, their ability to use the language beyond the classroom?

2. What strategies do I have in place for learners to self-assess? How are these practices having an impact on learning and motivation?

3. How do I know that my students are developing interculturality?

Chapter 5 | Curriculum Design

Learning to speak another's language means taking one's place in the human community. It means reaching out to others across cultural and linguistic boundaries. Language is far more than a system to be explained. It is our most important link to the world around us. Language is culture in motion. It is people interacting with people.

— *Sandra Savignon*

Figure 14. Curriculum Design for Learning Languages in the 21st Century with Global Themes

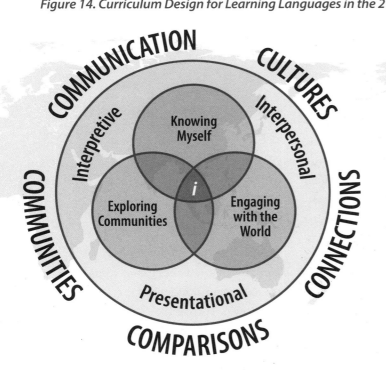

Belonging

Challenges

Creativity

Discovery

Exploring Time and Place

Identity

Well-Being

What Does a Curriculum for Learning Languages Look Like in the 21st Century?

Mindset for Curriculum Design. Mickan (2013) states, "A curriculum is an inventory of what is to be taught and how it will be taught and assessed for the realization of particular goals . . . a selection of content, resources, and activities organized and sequenced for consistency and continuity of instruction" (pp. 24–25). Figure 14 (previously shown as Figure 6) serves as a visual reminder of the curriculum mindset that has been discussed in this publication. An effective curriculum must bring all required elements together to create an articulated scope and sequence that allows learners to advance to the highest possible levels of proficiency given the type of program. The documents need to be written in a format that is easily understood and accessible to teachers. Enduring understandings offer a starting point for curriculum development.

Enduring Understandings. As teachers we want to ensure that our learners retain the big ideas—the enduring understandings. For that to happen, we must focus on ideas that have value beyond the classroom, those that are at the heart of our discipline. Wiggins and McTighe (2005) state that an enduring understanding may provide a conceptual foundation for basic skills: "All skills derive their value from the strategic principles that help us know when and how to use the skill" (p. 115). As stated previously, the overarching enduring understanding for all language learning is based on the goal statement in *Standards for Foreign Language Learning in the 21st Century* (NSFLEP, 2006): "To study another language and culture gives one the powerful key to successful communication: *knowing how, when, and why, to say what to whom*" (p. 11). Developing our discipline-specific enduring understandings challenges us to determine what it is that we want our learners to remember long after they have left our classrooms. Enduring understandings based on the Standards give direction to all programs no matter what the structure of a particular program might be. The goal areas of the Standards—Communication, Cultures, Connections, Comparisons, and Communities—are implicit in the enduring understandings that follow:

- Knowledge of another language fosters a better understanding of one's own language and culture, allowing for development of interculturality.

- Communicating in another language is a vehicle to gain knowledge and understandings that can only be acquired through that language and its culture(s).
- Learning other languages enables an individual to participate in multilingual communities locally and globally.

Themes, Topics, and Essential Questions. As discussed in Chapter 2, themes, topics, and essential questions provide the structure necessary to create an articulated program model. Working with different themes at different times and with topics that are increasingly more complex creates an articulated curriculum. This type of planning allows all programs to create a viable curriculum that is appropriate for their setting. Begin by creating a plan showing when learners will encounter certain themes and topics, identifying potential essential questions that will anchor the thematic units. Figure 15 shows how one such unit is created. Once teachers have agreed, they can begin over time to create the thematic units that will be used in the program.

Figure 15. Theme, Topic and Essential Question

There are clear advantages to using such an approach. The themes reoccur throughout the years and teachers can determine how to recycle topics in more complex ways, allowing learners to build on what has been previously learned. One sample progression is shown in Table 52.

A chart showing sample essential questions for each of the 21st Century Global Themes is found in Appendix G.

Text Type. The ACTFL Proficiency Guidelines and Performance Descriptors for Language Learners both explain the progression that learners make as they move from words to narration and description within a paragraph. Figure 16 captures this progression from Novice to Advanced using text type as the organizing principle. Text type can be used

Table 52. Theme and Essential Questions

Theme	Novice	Intermediate	Advanced
Discovery	Who are the inventors?	How are advances in science impacting my life today?	What inventions are needed to improve the quality of life on earth?

to explain in simple, concrete terms how learners use increasingly more complex language over time.

Figure 16. Text Type from Novice to Advanced

words   memorized sentences   sample sentences   strings of sentences   paragraphs

Top Ten Functions

Teachers now have the content and contexts (theme, topic, and essential question) for what they will teach and an understanding of how text type can be used to develop a progression for language learning. Now, let's consider the role that language functions play in the curriculum planning process. The thematic unit plan introduced in Chapter 2 required that language functions be identified as part of the Toolbox. These language functions are key to developing competency in another language. A list of possible language functions is available as a reference (see Appendix K). By looking at the list, it is easy to see that some functions are used more frequently than others. It is suggested that the following 10 high-frequency functions be revisited by learners multiple times as they build their language skills toward greater proficiency:

- Asking and responding to questions;
- Describing people, places, things;
- Expressing feelings and emotions;
- Expressing preferences and opinions;
- Maintaining a conversation or discussion in person or virtually;
- Telling or retelling stories;
- Summarizing authentic oral text;
- Interpreting authentic written text;
- Presenting information orally; and
- Presenting information in writing.

By combining these 10 functions with the text type progression shown in Figure 16, it is possible to create a curriculum spiral where learners return to the same high-frequency functions while increasing the complexity of the function each time. Sharing this information with learners allows them to monitor their progress in very concrete ways. The functions and progression based on text type are shown in Table 53.

Table 53. Moving Toward Proficiency

	Novice		Intermediate		Advanced
Asking and responding to questions	Respond to a simple question	Ask and respond to simple, memorized questions	Ask and respond with details to who, what, when, and why questions	Maintain a conversation, asking and responding to questions and follow-up questions	Sustain a conversation, asking and responding to detailed questions with follow-ups
Describing people, places, things	Describe using one or two words	Describe using short sentences	Describe using many adjectives	Use a variety of descriptors in several long sentences	Give precise and detailed descriptions of paragraph length
Expressing feelings and emotions	Say that I am happy or sad	Express my emotions in simple sentences	Express emotions such as surprise, happiness, anger, and sadness with some explanation	Express and react to a variety of emotions and feelings, giving detailed explanations	Clearly clarify my emotions and feelings using precise vocabulary and detailed explanations
Expressing preferences and opinions	When asked, I can respond with "I like/don't like it"	Ask and respond to questions about likes and dislikes	Share with someone my personal preferences and opinions with simple reasons	Share with someone my personal preferences and opinions, offering detailed explanations to support my opinions	Provide a detailed rationale or argument to support my opinion on a wide variety of topics
Maintaining a conversation in person or virtually	Exchange greetings/farewells	Participate in a short conversation on very familiar topics	Carry on a conversation on a variety of topics that are familiar to me	Initiate and maintain a conversation with ease and confidence on a variety of topics	Sustain a conversation on a wide variety of topics and appropriately handle an unexpected event or complication
Telling or retelling stories	Say what I am doing in short memorized sentences	Tell someone about my day in short, simple sentences	Tell a story in a series of sentences	Tell about something that happened or will happen giving the sequence of events	Tell a detailed story using paragraph-length narration to describe the event
Summarizing authentic oral text	identify a few words I have heard frequently	respond appropriately to simple, short announcements or directions	describe the main ideas of a radio/television program, movie, or podcast on a familiar topic	summarize the main idea and several supporting details of a radio/television program, movie, or podcast	analyze the contents of a radio/television program, movie, or podcast
Interpreting authentic written text	identify a few words I have learned	respond appropriately to a short note or message that uses very familiar words I have learned	describe the main ideas and some inferences of a literary or informational text that includes visuals	summarize the main idea, several details, and inferences of a literary or informational text on a familiar topic	analyze in detail a literary or informational text
Presenting information orally	introduce self or a topic using simple memorized information	give short presentations on personal experiences or very familiar topics	give information or explanation on a topic of personal interest	give a speech to persuade or explain	present a detailed, researched report on an academic topic
Presenting information in writing	list information using simple memorized sentences	express thoughts in a note or message	describe with simple details a person, event or experience	create a narrative of an experience or event	present a detailed, researched report on an academic topic

Curriculum Overview

Certainly, learners will work with other functions in various units and teachers may decide that there are additional functions of equal importance to those that are presented here. What is most important is that key functions are identified, allowing both teachers and learners to know the primary functions that anchor a curriculum sequence.

An effective curriculum document pulls elements of curriculum, instruction and assessment together in a format that is easily understood and accessible to teachers. The curriculum document makes it possible for busy teachers to make informed decisions about instruction and assessment on a regular basis. The format suggested here strives to capture the essential details in a way that allows busy teachers to see key details at a glance. The unit template presented in Chapter 2 then gives additional details for each unit in a particular grade or course. Table 54 shows what a curriculum overview might

Table 54. Curriculum Overview

Language: French Level: Novice Mid–Novice High						
Unit 1	**Summative Performance Assessments**			**Toolbox**		
	Theme/Topic/ Essential Question	**Interpretive**	**Presentational**	**Language Functions**	**Structures/ Patterns**	**Vocabulary Expansion**
	Well-Being: A Balanced Lifestyle How do people here and in (the French-speaking world) describe a balanced lifestyle?	• read a blog written by a teenager where he discusses his activities • watch a commercial for a product that promises to make life easier or less stressful • read a schedule of a top athlete to determine how he spends the hours in his day	• create a presentation based on multiple sources of information, highlighting ways to promote a balanced lifestyle for teenagers; share with another French class.	• exchange what they have learned about their lifestyle and the lifestyle of teenagers in (France) in terms of a balanced lifestyle; compare their daily routines and schedules and make and respond to suggestions to adjust their lifestyle	• Compare lifestyle routines • Describe your daily schedule • Ask and answer questions about daily routines • Express frequency, saying when and how often you do certain things • Express needs, saying what you need to do to be healthy • Express opinions about daily activities, schedules • Make suggestions about ways to be healthy	• *plus que, moins plus que, moins que, aussi que* (more than, less than, as… as) • *(le) lundi…* (on Mondays) • interrogative pronouns and adjectives • adverbs • *Il faut/Il me faut* (It's necessary/I need) • *Il est important de, Il est bon de* (It's important to/it's good to) • *Tu devrais/Vous devriez* • *Il te/vous faut* (You should/you need to)	**Tier 1** • sports, activities • expressions/ adverbs of frequency **Tier 2** • *Une bonne hygiène de vie* (a healthy lifestyle) • *Un régime équilibré* (a balanced diet) • *La détente* (relaxation) • *s'entraîner* (to exercise) • *Se détendre/ se dépêcher* (to relax/to hurry) • *Être détendu/ être stressé* (to be relaxed/to be stressed)
Unit 2	**Summative Performance Assessments**			**Toolbox**		
	Theme/Topic/ Essential Question	**Interpretive**	**Presentational**	**Language Functions**	**Structures/ Patterns**	**Vocabulary Expansion**

look like, providing a basic building block for the curriculum map for an entire language program.

Teachers can see at a glance the units for a particular course or level. The theme, topic, and essential question appear in the overview. The unit goals are reflected in the summative performance assessments that anchor the unit. Key elements of the unit Toolbox are also part of the curriculum overview. The language functions are listed with the structures and patterns that are needed to support those functions and teachers can also see the vocabulary that students will need to meet the goals of the unit. Teachers would still refer to the unit template for additional details on how the unit addressed the Standards, for key learning activities, resources and for suggestions for technology integration. The overview is formatted so that all of the units for a given level or course fit on a page allowing teachers easy visual access to the horizontal and vertical curriculum of any program. This overview is also available at www.actfl.org/publications/books-and-brochures/the-keys-planning-learning. With everything in place for an articulated curriculum, let's consider two final questions.

How Many Units Should I Teach Each Year? The number of units really depends on the actual teaching situation and arguments could easily be made for a certain number of units in any given situation. School calendars and grading cycles could affect the number of units. A typical high school system with four quarters and four grading periods might want to teach five or six units, making certain that units never end during the last week of a grading period. An elementary class that meets twice a week for 25 minutes might opt for only two or three units a year to create continuity of topic given the limited number of contact minutes. Beyond the practical considerations of the school calendar, think about the impact on student learning. How much time will teachers and learners need for meeting unit goals? If learners are to meet unit goals successfully, they will need time to develop their skills within each mode of communication. Learners need time to acquire new vocabulary and new structures that are used in meaningful contexts as they discuss, acquire, and present the ideas of the unit. They will need time to surface their own questions and time to explore those questions. They will need time to create their products in the presentational mode, to revise their work in collaboration with others and to share those final products. Teachers need time to work with individual learners to create opportunities for feedback at critical points in the unit. The most frequently

voiced concern in terms of curriculum is that there is never enough time. As thematic units are implemented, teachers are empowered to make more efficient use of time in ways that empower student learning.

What About Grammar? At this point, some readers are surely asking themselves about grammar. Remember that every language function requires key structures. The Toolbox for the thematic unit required that functions be listed first followed by the structures associated with those functions. This places grammar in the appropriate context. It is presented and addressed when it is needed for specific communicative purposes. This intentional placement allows teachers and learners to focus on what is essential—the ability to communicate a message to an intended audience. The intentional spiral that occurs as certain key functions are revisited also allows the supporting structures to be reintegrated and allows for increased control of specific structures over time. With recognition that full control does not come early in the process, teachers and learners benefit by knowing that errors are a natural part of the language learning process. Crockett advocates a culture where error correction is replaced by encouragement and praise for communicating a message and adds that the result is a classroom where the culture is warmer and more welcoming (in Zilmer, 2013). This does not mean that there is no need for error correction; rather, error correction occurs at appropriate moments.

This chapter presented details that must be considered in the development of a well-articulated scope and sequence for a world language program. While a publication is limited to what can be conveyed in print, we believe that the templates and overviews presented here will transfer easily to the numerous electronic curriculum tools that are in use today. Without a doubt, there is a great deal of energy, thoughtfulness, creativity, and time involved in developing a curriculum with units and lessons that allow learners to reach program goals and, more importantly, their personal goals. The creativity involved in curriculum development is most certainly the same process that creates a great work of art.

A great piece of art is composed not just of what is in the final piece, but equally important, what is not. It is the discipline to discard what does not fit—to cut out what might have already cost days or even years of effort—that distinguishes the truly exceptional artist and marks the ideal piece of work, be it a symphony, a novel, a painting, a company or, most important of all, a life.

(Collins, 2003)

Application

1. You are the designated mentor to a new colleague. You need to explain your program goals. What would you say? What documents would you share? How do you explain how well prepared the learners should be at the end of the course they are taking?

2. You and your department members are ready to make some changes. You want to teach fewer units and place more emphasis on student performance. What rationale would you share with administration to convince them to offer time and/or funding for curriculum development work?

Reflection

1. How do I address key functions throughout the curriculum? What functions do I need to add to the Top 10 list to meet my program goals?

2. Given that I have a limited amount of time, what is a logical next step for me in terms of curriculum, unit, and lesson design?

Final Thoughts
For Ongoing Reflection

We opened this publication on curriculum, unit, and lesson design by describing the 21st century learner and teacher. We described the learner as "hyper-connected to the world" and ready to explore multiple sources of information almost simultaneously with the click of a button. We described the 21st century teacher as a facilitator, providing space, time, and guidance to learners as they traveled the world from their laptop, tablet, or smartphone. In the 21st century, educators are tasked not with teaching learners *what* to think, but rather with teaching learners *how* to think. Technology is truly the bridgebuilder of the 21st century, connecting people around the world. The 21st Century Skills of Communication, Critical Thinking, Creativity, and, most importantly, Collaboration are essential skills for all learners. The language classroom is the ideal place to bring all those skills together for global collaboration.

Classrooms and schools in the United States are connecting with classrooms and schools around the world to discuss issues of importance that transcend boundaries. The 21st century learner is also connecting as an individual through social networks. "Learning is social"—that statement has never been truer than it is today. Learners who live in rural areas no longer have to feel isolated. The world is just a click away. Furthermore, language learners have the advantage of being able to click and connect in more than one language. Think of the possibilities!

Let's return to our original question: What does a curriculum for learning languages look like in the 21st century? First and foremost, it is flexible and encourages learners to be curious about the global community in which they live. With flexibility in mind, we have selected seven global themes—Belonging, Challenges, Creativity, Discovery, Exploring Time and Place, Identity and Well-Being—designed as lenses through which learners can simultaneously learn about people, places, and cultures around the world as they learn about themselves. While there are no prescribed topics within the themes, the 5 Cs of the Standards for Learning Languages—Communication, Cultures, Connections, Comparisons, and Communities—give depth and breadth to the content. In fact, the beauty of the global themes is that they can be interpreted in a multitude of ways. You may recall that in describing the unit on a balanced lifestyle, we showed how it could be connected to all of the seven themes, depending on how learners wanted to explore the topic.

Second, the 21st century language learning curriculum encourages curiosity. With that goal in mind, we encouraged unit planning around a theme and topic, and an essential question related to that theme and topic. Because the themes are intentionally broad, we felt it important to encourage unit designers to focus on a topic related to the theme as an intermediary step to the more important step of designing an essential question to guide the learning in the unit of study. In the 21st century language classroom, learners should determine questions and ultimately the essential question they want to explore as a way to foster their natural curiosity about the world. We know that motivation is essential to the learning process. How better to motivate learners than by putting them in the driver's seat, letting them ask questions and then having them connect with people around the world to find answers?

Third, the 21st century language learning curriculum requires global collaboration. There are not enough creative and innovative ideas in any one classroom to address all of the challenges facing today's global citizens. The challenges are complex and require people of diverse backgrounds to bring their perspectives and knowledge to a virtual roundtable. Language learners need highly developed skills in interculturality to make those virtual discussions successful collaborations. Again, language learners are uniquely poised to be leaders in these discussions because they have grappled with the intricacies of communicating effectively with people from other cultures. Kramsch (1993) expressed the importance of teaching culture in language classes:

> Culture in language teaching is not an expendable fifth skill, tacked on, so to speak, to the teaching of speaking, listening, reading, and writing. It is always in the background, right from day one, ready to unsettle the good language learners when they expect it least, making evident the limitations of their hard-won communicative competence, challenging their ability to make sense of the world around them (p. 8).

We cannot prepare language learners for successful global collaboration unless we emphasize that learning a language is learning a culture. Fallows (2010) in the book, *Dreaming in Chinese*, eloquently expresses how language and culture are inextricably linked:

> I often found a connection between some point of the language—a particular word or the use of a phrase, for example—and how that point could elucidate something very "Chinese" I would encounter in my everyday life in China. The language helped me understand what I saw on the streets or on our travels around the country—how people made their livings, their habits, their behavior toward each other, how they dealt with adversity, and how they celebrated. This book is the story of what I learned about the Chinese language, and what the language taught me about China (p. 15).

Finally, the 21st century language teacher, just like teachers of all disciplines, is teaching learners *how* to learn and not *what* to learn. The pathway to proficiency guides language learners to continuously expand their understanding and communication skills in an expanding number of contexts, beginning with words, phrases, memorized sentences, and questions, and branching out to express their own ideas by creating with language in longer sentences and questions, eventually moving to paragraph-length narration. Learners who reach that level of proficiency and who seek to continue to develop their linguistic and cultural skills will be well-prepared to take their place in a global society.

We would like to leave you with this vision for language study:

To prepare young people for meaningful interactions with people around the world, helping them understand the inextricable link between language and culture as they work to understand and communicate with respect in the language they are learning, and, at the same time, deepening their understanding of their own language and culture; to prepare young people to be explorers: being curious, asking questions, being open to sharing new experiences and new ideas, ultimately with the goal of creating networks of collaboration to address the challenges facing today's world.

Appendix A | World-Readiness Standards for Learning Languages (2013)

Communication

Communicate effectively in more than one language in order to function in a variety of situations and for multiple purposes.

Interpersonal Communication: Learners interact and negotiate meaning in spoken, signed, or written conversations to share information, reactions, feelings, and opinions.

Interpretive Communication: Learners understand, interpret, and analyze what is heard, read, or viewed on a variety of topics.

Presentational Communication: Learners present information, concepts, and ideas to inform, explain, persuade, and narrate on a variety of topics using appropriate media and adapting to various audiences of listeners, readers, or viewers.

Cultures

Interact with cultural competence and understanding.

Relating Cultural Practices to Perspectives: Learners use the language to investigate, explain, and reflect on the relationship between the practices and perspectives of the cultures studied.

Relating Cultural Products to Perspectives: Learners use the language to investigate, explain, and reflect on the relationship between the products and perspectives of the cultures studied.

Connections

Connect with other disciplines and acquire information and diverse perspectives in order to use the language to function in academic and career-related situations.

Making Connections: Learners build, reinforce, and expand their knowledge of other disciplines while using the language to develop critical thinking and to solve problems creatively.

Acquiring Information and Diverse Perspectives: Learners access and evaluate information and diverse perspectives that are available through the language and its cultures.

Comparisons

Develop insight into the nature of language and culture in order to interact with cultural competence.

Language Comparisons: Learners use the language to investigate, explain, and reflect on the nature of language through comparisons of the language studied and their own.

Cultural Comparisons: Learners use the language to investigate, explain, and reflect on the concept of culture through comparisons of the cultures studied and their own.

Communities

Communicate and interact with cultural competence in order to participate in multilingual communities at home and around the world.

School and Global Communities: Learners use the language both within and beyond the classroom to interact and collaborate in their community and the globalized world.

Lifelong Learning: Learners set goals and reflect on their progress in using languages for enjoyment, enrichment, and advancement.

Appendix B | ACTFL Proficiency Guidelines Summary

	Reading
Novice	Readers can understand key words and cognates, as well as formulaic phrases that are highly contextualized. They are able to get a limited amount of information from highly predictable texts in which the topic or context is very familiar, such as a weather map. They may rely heavily on their own background knowledge and extralinguistic support (such as the imagery on the weather map) to derive meaning. They are best able to understand a text when they are able to anticipate the information in the text. Recognition of key words, cognates, and formulaic phrases makes comprehension possible.
Intermediate	Readers can understand information conveyed in simple, predictable, loosely connected texts. They rely heavily on contextual clues. They can most easily understand information if the format of the text is familiar, such as in a weather report or a social announcement. They are able to understand texts that convey basic information such as that found in announcements, notices, and online bulletin boards and forums. These texts are non-complex and have a predictable pattern of presentation. The discourse is minimally connected and primarily organized in individual sentences and strings of sentences containing predominantly high-frequency vocabulary. They are most accurate when getting meaning from simple, straightforward texts. They are able to understand messages found in highly familiar, everyday contexts. They may not fully understand texts that are detailed or those texts in which knowledge of language structures is essential in order to understand sequencing, time frame, and chronology.
Advanced	Readers can understand the main idea and supporting details of authentic narrative and descriptive texts. They are able to compensate for limitations in their lexical and structural knowledge by using contextual clues. Comprehension is likewise supported by knowledge of the conventions of the language (e.g., noun/adjective agreement, verb placement, etc.). When familiar with the subject matter, readers are also able to derive some meaning from straightforward argumentative texts (e.g., recognizing the main argument). They are able to understand texts that have a clear and predictable structure. For the most part, the prose is uncomplicated and the subject matter pertains to real-world topics of general interest. They demonstrate an independence in their ability to read subject matter that is new to them. They have sufficient control of standard linguistic conventions to understand sequencing, time frames, and chronology. However, these readers are likely challenged by texts in which issues are treated abstractly.
	Listening
Novice	Listeners can understand key words, true aural cognates, and formulaic expressions that are highly contextualized and highly predictable, such as those found in introductions and basic courtesies. They understand words and phrases from simple questions, statements, and high-frequency commands. They typically require repetition, rephrasing, and/or a slowed rate of speech for comprehension. They rely heavily on extralinguistic support to derive meaning. They are most accurate when they are able to recognize speech that they can anticipate. In this way, these listeners tend to recognize rather than truly comprehend. Their listening is largely dependent on factors other than the message itself.
Intermediate	Listeners can understand information conveyed in simple, sentence-length speech on familiar or everyday topics. They are generally able to comprehend one utterance at a time while engaged in face-to-face conversations or in routine listening tasks such as understanding highly contextualized messages, straightforward announcements, or simple instructions and directions. They rely heavily on redundancy, restatement, paraphrasing, and contextual clues. They understand speech that conveys basic information. This speech is simple, minimally connected, and contains high-frequency vocabulary. They are most accurate in their comprehension when getting meaning from simple, straightforward speech. They are able to comprehend messages found in highly familiar everyday contexts. Intermediate listeners require a controlled listening environment where they hear what they may expect to hear.
Advanced	Listeners can understand the main ideas and most supporting details in connected discourse on a variety of general interest topics, such as news stories, explanations, instructions, anecdotes, or travelogue descriptions. They are able to compensate for limitations in their lexical and structural control of the language by using real-world knowledge and contextual clues. They may also derive some meaning from oral texts at higher levels if they possess significant familiarity with the topic or context. They understand speech that is authentic and connected. This speech is lexically and structurally uncomplicated. The discourse is straightforward and is generally organized in a clear and predictable way. They demonstrate the ability to comprehend language on a range of topics of general interest. They have sufficient knowledge of language structure to understand basic time-frame references. Nevertheless, their understanding is most often limited to concrete, conventional discourse.

Writing	
Novice	Writers at the Novice level are characterized by the ability to produce lists and notes, primarily by writing words and phrases. They can provide limited formulaic information on simple forms and documents. These writers can reproduce practiced material to convey the most simple messages. In addition, they can transcribe familiar words or phrases, copy letters of the alphabet or syllables of a syllabary, or reproduce basic characters with some accuracy.
Intermediate	Writers at the Intermediate level are characterized by the ability to meet practical writing needs, such as simple messages and letters, requests for information, and notes. In addition, they can ask and respond to simple questions in writing. These writers can create with the language and communicate simple facts and ideas in a series of loosely connected sentences on topics of personal interest and social needs. They write primarily in present time. At this level, writers use basic vocabulary and structures to express meaning that is comprehensible to those accustomed to the writing of non-natives.
Advanced	Writers at the Advanced level are characterized by the ability to write routine informal and some formal correspondence, as well as narratives, descriptions, and summaries of a factual nature. They can narrate and describe in the major time frames of past, present, and future, using paraphrasing and elaboration to provide clarity. Advanced-level writers produce connected discourse of paragraph length and structure. At this level, writers show good control of the most frequently used structures and generic vocabulary, allowing them to be understood by those unaccustomed to the writing of non-natives.
Speaking	
Novice	Novice-level speakers can communicate short messages on highly predictable, everyday topics that affect them directly. They do so primarily through the use of isolated words and phrases that have been encountered, memorized, and recalled. Novice-level speakers may be difficult to understand even by the most sympathetic interlocutors accustomed to non-native speech.
Intermediate	Speakers at the Intermediate level are distinguished primarily by their ability to create with the language when talking about familiar topics related to their daily life. They are able to recombine learned material in order to express personal meaning. Intermediate-level speakers can ask simple questions and can handle a straightforward survival situation. They produce sentence-level language, ranging from discrete sentences to strings of sentences, typically in present time. Intermediate-level speakers are understood by interlocutors who are accustomed to dealing with non-native learners of the language.
Advanced	Speakers at the Advanced level engage in conversation in a clearly participatory manner in order to communicate information on autobiographical topics, as well as topics of community, national, or international interest. The topics are handled concretely by means of narration and description in the major time frames of past, present, and future. These speakers can also deal with a social situation with an unexpected complication. The language of Advanced-level speakers is abundant, the oral paragraph being the measure of Advanced-level length and discourse. Advanced-level speakers have sufficient control of basic structures and generic vocabulary to be understood by native speakers of the language, including those unaccustomed to non-native speech.

Appendix C | Methods, Theories, and Approaches of Language Acquisition

Methods/Theories/ Approaches	Teacher	Student	Summary	Example: Teaching *Bonjour*/Hello
Grammar Translation	• uses authentic texts • explains grammar, vocabulary, and culture in native language • prepares grammar and vocabulary exercises	• reads silently • listens to explanations • memorizes words and rules • prepares written translations	Learners memorize the rules of the language in order to read and translate texts.	*"Bonjour" learned by vocabulary lists and by translating.* *Bonjour* = Hello Hello = *Bonjour*
Direct/Natural	• uses language actively in classroom • uses actions and demonstration to convey meaning • focuses on pronunciation • teaches grammar inductively	• repeats the language, correct pronunciation important • figures out grammar rules	Learners repeat and memorize oral dialogues. They ask and answer formulaic questions in class, work in language labs. Dictation is a common practice.	*"Bonjour" learned through numerous, frequent repetitions.* T: *Bonjour* S: *Bonjour*
ALM	• introduces dialogues that are typical of certain situations—post office, restaurant, etc.	• reads and repeats dialogues • memorizes dialogues	Learners memorize formal dialogues that do not capture authentic ways of speaking.	*"Bonjour" learned in numerous, frequent dialogues.* - *Bonjour*, Pierre. - *Bonjour*, Anne.
Functional– Notional	• selects topics relevant to learners' lives • determines function needed for topic • teaches grammar when it is needed	• interacts conversationally using functions and grammatical structure	Learners interact in realistic ways about topics of interest. Language is often constrained by requiring learners to use certain structures tied to functions.	*"Bonjour" becomes a way to meet and greet someone.*
Communicative Competency Proficiency-Based	• engages learners in conversation • creates scenarios to perform functions in a range of contexts • places focus on meaning and form	• participates in conversational role plays • attends to meaning and form	Learners use language in situations that approximate real-life, but are not always real to students.	*"Bonjour" becomes part of role-plays, games, and simulations.* Teacher gives the task: You are meeting a foreign exchange student for the first time. Greet him or her.

Methods/Theories	Teacher Approach	Student Activities	Summary	Example: Teaching *Bonjour*/Hello
Total Physical Response **Total Proficiency Through Reading and Storytelling**	• develops comprehension before speech • gives commands in the target language • makes use of gestures, and physical action to convey meaning • creates and shares stories using previously learned vocabulary	• infers meaning from commands and stories • acts out commands • acts out stories • retells story; creates own versions of stories by recombining learned elements	Learners demonstrate comprehension by their actions and responses. They are able to recombine elements to create personal stories.	*"Bonjour" is acted out or becomes part of a story.* Student hears *Bonjour* and waves hand. Student creates a story that incorporates *Bonjour*.
Task-Based **Project-Based**	• develops tasks that require learner to use target language to meet a specific objective • designs task for use of selected grammar and vocabulary items	• negotiates meaning to understand others • uses language to complete tasks	Learners complete tasks, but may be able to do so without use of the target language or by avoiding intended linguistic structures and vocabulary.	*"Bonjour" is an element of a task.* Teacher assigns task: You will be welcoming visitors from various countries. Design a multimedia, print, and audio campaign that greets everyone appropriately.
Content-Based	• uses the target language 100% of the time • teaches grade-level content • integrates language skills as content is taught	• learns content in the target language • uses language skills to demonstrate comprehension of content	Learners use language to access and understand content while developing increased language skills.	*"Bonjour" is not necessarily part of the unit.* *Bonjour* may or may not be learned as students work with the life cycle of a butterfly in science class.
Sociocultural	• uses authentic text as cultural artifacts • focuses on culturally respectful communication • plans tasks that allow learners to perform beyond current ability but within the Zone of Proximal Development (Vygotsky)	• develops language skills by interacting with others • work extensively with authentic text • attends to cultural and communicative competence	Learners engage with language by working with concepts, language, and symbols in ways that language speakers do.	*"Bonjour" occurs in an authentic situation (e.g., learners may watch a movie).* Learners interact with authentic text to learn *Bonjour*.

Based on information from Horowitz (2008), Mickan (2013), and Shrum and Glisan (2010).

Appendix D | Education Unit

Language and Level/Grade:	French – Novice High ➜ Intermediate Low	Approximate Length:	6 weeks
		Approximate Number of Minutes Weekly:	250 minutes

Theme/Topic	Challenges: Education
Essential Question	Why can't all young people go to school?

Goals *What should learners know and be able to do by the end of the unit?*	Learners will be able to: • describe the current status of education of young people locally, nationally, and globally • identify and categorize economic, political, and social reasons why young people around the world cannot go to/stay in school • give reasons why going to school is important to oneself and locally, nationally, and globally • give examples of initiatives to support schooling for all young people around the world • connect with a school in (x) to learn more about the school; collaborate to develop a plan for continued communication

Summative Performance Assessment • *These tasks allow learners to demonstrate how well they have met the goals of the unit.* • *They are integrated throughout the unit.* • *The template encourages multiple interpretive tasks.* • *The interpretive tasks inform the content of the presentational and interpersonal tasks.* • *The tasks incorporate 21st Century Skills.*	**Interpretive Mode**	
	Learners watch a movie about a young girl in Senegal who cannot go to school. Afterwards, the learners will list the reasons that she cannot go to school based on the film, and evaluate the accuracy of the film based on background information on why children cannot go to school.	Learners read an article giving reasons why all children should go to school. They categorize the reasons given by completing a graphic organizer.
	Presentational Mode	**Interpersonal Mode**
	Learners work in groups to design a plan for continued collaboration with a school in (x); groups share their plan with other groups in class in order to select one plan to pursue.	After the class selects a plan, learners will meet in small groups to discuss that plan. They will decide how to implement the plan and how to involve other classes/schools/community in the collaboration.

Cultures (Sample Evidence) *Indicate the relationship between the product, practice, and perspective.*	**Product:** School **Practice:** Going to School **Perspective:** Importance of school for all young people in (x) **Product:** Daily class schedule **Practice:** Required vs. elective courses **Perspective:** Purpose of school

Connections (Sample Evidence)	**Making Connections**	**Acquiring Information and Diverse Perspectives**
	Social Studies: • Education as the right of the child (United Nations) • Global challenge of educating all young people **English Language Arts:** • Synthesis of information from a variety of sources • Sharing information and ideas with others through discussions	Education systems and practices around the world and reasons for those systems and practices

Comparisons (Sample Evidence)	**Language Comparisons**	**Cultural Comparisons**
	• *une année blanche* (a missed year) • *passer le bac* (to take the *bac*)	• Reasons to attend/not attend school • Exams in high school

Communities (Sample Evidence)	School and Global Communities	Lifelong Learning
	Inform others about education around the world and opportunities for collaboration on a project related to education for all.	Consider the role that education plays in your life and set personal goals.
Connections to Common Core	**Writing: 6.** Use technology, including the Internet, to produce and publish writing and to interact and collaborate with others. **Speaking and Listening: 1.** Prepare for and participate effectively in a range of conversations and collaborations with diverse partners, building on others' ideas and expressing their own clearly and persuasively. **Speaking and Listening: 2.** Integrate and evaluate information presented in diverse media and formats, including visually, quantitatively, and orally.	

Toolbox		
Language Functions	**Related Structures/Patterns**	**Vocabulary Expansion** **Tier 1**
Compare *various components of school systems/ schedules*	*plus de, moins de, autant de* (more of, less of, as much of)	school subjects
Describe *attitudes toward attending school*	*Il est important que, Il est nécessaire que, il est dommage que, afin que, pour que* (It's important that, it's necessary that, it's too bad that, so that, in order that)	**Tier 2** *Les droits de l'enfant* (rights of the child) *Manquer de formation* (lack training/schooling) *Aller à l'école* (to go to school)
Express opinions *on the importance of school*	*Il est important que, Il est nécessaire que, il est dommage que, afin que, pour que* (It's important that, it's necessary that, it's too bad that, so that, in order that)	*Assister aux cours* (to attend classes) *Réussir/échouer* (to pass/to fail) *Relier/Partager/Echanger* (to connect, to share, to exchange) *L'alphabétisation* (literacy)
Ask and answer questions *to learn more about schooling in other cultures*	Interrogatives	*Obligatoire/facultatif* (required/optional) *Interdit/permis* (forbidden/allowed)

Key Learning Activity/Formative Assessment			
Key Learning Activity/ Formative Assessment *(representative samples from beginning to end of unit)*	**How does this activity support the unit goals or performance tasks?**	**Mode of Communication**	**Interculturality S**elf **C**ommunity **W**orld
Small groups: brainstorm why we have schools	Introduce the role and importance of school	Interpersonal	S, C, W
Listen to song *Sacre Charlemagne*: identify who invented schools according to the song; determine attitude toward school in song	Provide background information on school	Interpretive	C
Read short biography of Charlemagne and his view on the importance of education	Provide historic context for schools	Interpretive	C
Read *"l'histoire de l'école"* and create a timeline of important dates related to schools www.copaindumonde.org/5136.0.HTML	Provide historic context for schools	Interpretive, Presentational	C
Compare school systems in various countries around the world	Provide information on schools	Interpretive, Presentational	C,W
Small groups: brainstorm reasons why all young people locally, nationally, or internationally can't go to school	Assess background knowledge	Interpersonal	S, C, W
Read www.copaindumonde.org/5145.0.html and list the current situation related to children's rights to school.	Provide current information on schooling	Interpretive	
View film explaining the importance of education for all children at www.YouTube.com/watch?v=Ol3eK2r75T8= ; afterwards discuss in small groups the degree to which you agree with the film's perspective	Viewpoint on why education is important	Interpretive, Interpersonal	W
View prezi.com/_9icbrqc-uhg/education-counts/	Provide global context	Interpretive	W

Resources	Technology Integration
La Petite Vendeuse de Soleil – film about girl in Sénégal World Wise Schools website about education: • wws.peacecorps.gov/wws/educators/lessonplans/lesson.cfm?lpid=3578 Film explaining importance of education for all children: • www.youtube.com/watch?v=Ol3eK2r75T8 Additional resources available at: • www.actfl.org/publications/books-and-brochures/the-keys-planning-learning	• www.epals.com allows you to connect with classrooms around the world • www.skype.com allows you to connect with others via live video • www.education.weebly.com allows you to create an interactive website

Appendix E | ACTFL Performance Descriptors for Language Learners

ACTFL Performance Descriptors For Language Learners–Presentational

Domains	Novice Range	Intermediate Range	Advanced Range
	Communicates information on very familiar topics using a variety of words, phrases, and sentences that have been practiced and memorized.	Communicates information and expresses own thoughts about familiar topics using sentences and series of sentences.	Communicates information and expresses self with detail and organization on familiar and some new concrete topics using paragraphs.
Functions	Presents simple, basic information on very familiar topics by producing words, lists, notes and formulaic language using highly practiced language. May show emerging evidence of the ability to express own thoughts and preferences.	Expresses own thoughts and presents information and personal preferences on familiar topics by creating with language primarily in present time. May show emerging evidence of the ability to tell or retell a story and provide additional description.	Produces narrations and descriptions in all major time frames on familiar and some unfamiliar topics. May show emerging evidence of the ability to provide a well-supported argument, including detailed evidence in support of a point of view.
Contexts/ Content	Creates messages in some personally relevant contexts on topics that relate to basic biographical information. May show emerging evidence of the ability to create messages in highly practiced contexts related to oneself and immediate environment.	Creates messages in contexts relevant to oneself, others, and one's immediate environment. May show emerging evidence of the ability to create messages on general interest and work-related topics.	Creates messages fully and effectively in contexts both personal and general. Content areas include topics of personal and general interest (community, national, and international events) as well as work-related topics and areas of special competence. May show emerging evidence of the ability to create messages in more abstract content areas.
Text Type	Produces words and phrases and highly practiced sentences or formulaic questions.	Produces sentences, series of sentences, and some connected sentences.	Produces full paragraphs that are organized and detailed.
Language Control	Produces memorized language that is appropriate to the context; limited language control may require a sympathetic audience to be understood. With practice, polish, or editing, may show emerging evidence of Intermediate-level language control.	Control of language is sufficient to be understood by audiences accustomed to the language produced by language learners. With practice, polish, or editing, may show emerging evidence of Advanced-level language control.	Control of high-frequency structures is sufficient to be understood by audiences not accustomed to the language of language learners. With practice, polish, or editing, shows evidence of Advanced-level control of grammar and syntax.
Vocabulary	Produces a number of high frequency words and formulaic expressions; able to use a limited variety of vocabulary on familiar topics.	Produces vocabulary on a variety of everyday topics, topics of personal interest, and topics that have been studied.	Produces a broad range of vocabulary related to topics of personal, public, and community interest, and some specific vocabulary related to areas of study or expertise.
Communication Strategies	May use some or all of the following strategies to communicate, able to: • Rely on a practiced format • Use facial expressions and gestures • Repeat words • Resort to first language • Use graphic organizers to present information • Rely on multiple drafts and practice sessions with feedback • Support presentational speaking with visuals and notes • Support presentational writing with visuals or prompts	May use some or all of the following strategies to communicate and maintain audience interest, able to: • Show an increasing awareness of errors and able to self-correct or edit • Use phrases, imagery, or content • Simplify • Use known language to compensate for missing vocabulary • Use graphic organizer • Use reference resources as appropriate	May use some or all of the following strategies to communicate and maintain audience interest, able to: • Demonstrate conscious efforts at self-editing and correction • Elaborate and clarify • Provide examples, synonyms, or antonyms • Use cohesion, chronology, and details to explain or narrate fully • Circumlocute
Cultural Awareness	May use some memorized culturally appropriate gestures, formulaic expressions, and basic writing conventions.	Uses some culturally appropriate vocabulary, expressions, and gestures. Reflects some knowledge of cultural differences related to written and spoken communication.	Uses cultural knowledge appropriate to the presentational context and increasingly reflective of authentic cultural practices and perspectives.

ACTFL Performance Descriptors For Language Learners–Interpersonal

Domains	Novice Range	Intermediate Range	Advanced Range
	Expresses self in conversations on very familiar topics using a variety of words, phrases, simple sentences, and questions that have been highly practiced and memorized.	Expresses self and participates in conversations on familiar topics using sentences and series of sentences. Handles short social interactions in everyday situations by asking and answering a variety of questions. Can communicate about self, others, and everyday life.	Expresses self fully to maintain conversations on familiar topics and new concrete social, academic, and work-related topics. Can communicate in paragraph-length conversation about events with detail and organization. Confidently handles situations with an unexpected complication. Shares point of view in discussions.
Functions	Can ask highly predictable and formulaic questions and respond to such questions by listing, naming, and identifying. May show emerging evidence of the ability to engage in simple conversation	Can communicate by understanding and creating personal meaning. Can understand, ask, and answer a variety of questions. Consistently able to initiate, maintain, and end a conversation to satisfy basic needs and/or to handle a simple transaction. May show emerging evidence of the ability to communicate about more than the "here and now."	Can communicate with ease and confidence by understanding and producing narrations and descriptions in all major time frames and deal efficiently with a situation with an unexpected turn of events. May show emerging evidence of the ability to participate in discussions about issues beyond the concrete.
Contexts/ Content	Able to function in some personally relevant contexts on topics that relate to basic biographical information. May show emerging evidence of the ability to communicate in highly practiced contexts related to oneself and immediate environment.	Able to communicate in contexts relevant to oneself and others, and one's immediate environment. May show emerging evidence of the ability to communicate in contexts of occasionally unfamiliar topics.	Functions fully and effectively in contexts both personal and general. Content areas include topics of personal and general interest (community, national, and international events) as well as work-related topics and areas of special competence. May show emerging evidence of the ability to communicate in more abstract content areas.
Text Type	Understands and produces highly practiced words and phrases and an occasional sentence. Able to ask formulaic or memorized questions.	Able to understand and produce discrete sentences, strings of sentences, and some connected sentences. Able to ask questions to initiate and sustain conversations.	Able to understand and produce discourse in full oral paragraphs that are organized, cohesive, and detailed. Able to ask questions to probe beyond basic details.
Language Control	Can usually comprehend highly practiced and basic messages when supported by visual or contextual clues, redundancy or restatement, and when the message contains familiar structures. Can control memorized language sufficiently to be appropriate to the context and understood by those accustomed to dealing with language learners, however at times with difficulty.	Understands straightforward language that contains mostly familiar structures. Control of language is sufficient to be understood by those accustomed to dealing with language learners.	Language control is sufficient to interact efficiently and effectively with those unaccustomed to dealing with language learners. Consistent control of basic high-frequency structures facilitates comprehension and production.
Vocabulary	Able to understand and produce a number of high frequency words, highly practiced expressions, and formulaic questions.	Communicates using high frequency and personalized vocabulary within familiar themes or topics.	Comprehends and produces a broad range of vocabulary related to school, employment, topics of personal interest, and generic vocabulary related to current events and matters of public and community interest.
Communication Strategies	May use some or all of the following strategies to maintain communication, able to: • Imitate modeled words • Use facial expressions and gestures • Repeat words • Resort to first language • Ask for repetition • Indicate lack of understanding.	Uses some of the following strategies to maintain communication, but not all of the time and inconsistently, able to: • Ask questions • Ask for clarification • Self-correct or restate when not understood • Circumlocute	Uses a range of strategies to maintain communication, able to: • Request clarification • Repeat • Restate • Rephrase • Circumlocute
Cultural Awareness	May use culturally appropriate gestures and formulaic expressions in highly practiced applications. May show awareness of the most obvious cultural differences or prohibitions, but may often miss cues indicating miscommunication.	Recognizes and uses some culturally appropriate vocabulary, expressions, and gestures when participating in everyday interactions. Recognizes that differences exist in cultural behaviors and perspectives and can conform in familiar situations.	Understands and uses cultural knowledge to conform linguistically and behaviorally in many social and work-related interactions. Shows conscious awareness of significant cultural differences and attempts to adjust accordingly.

ACTFL Performance Descriptors For Language Learners–Interpretive

Domains	Novice Range	Intermediate Range	Advanced Range
	Understands words, phrases, and formulaic language that have been practiced and memorized to get meaning of the main idea from simple, highly-predictable oral or written texts, with strong visual support.	Understands main ideas and some supporting details on familiar topics from a variety of texts.	Understands main ideas and supporting details on familiar and some new, concrete topics from a variety of more complex texts that have a clear, organized structure.
Functions	Comprehends meaning through recognition of key words and formulaic phrases that are highly contextualized. May show emerging evidence of the ability to make inferences based on background and prior knowledge.	Comprehends main ideas and identifies some supporting details. May show emerging evidence of the ability to make inferences by identifying key details from the text.	Comprehends the main idea and supporting details of narrative, descriptive, and straightforward persuasive texts. Makes inferences and derives meaning from context and linguistic features.
Contexts/ Content	Comprehends texts with highly predictable, familiar contexts (those related to personal background, prior knowledge, or experiences).	Comprehends information related to basic personal and social needs and relevant to one's immediate environment such as self and everyday life, school, community, and particular interests.	Comprehends texts pertaining to real-world topics of general interest relevant to personal, social, work-related, community, national, and international contexts.
Text Type	Derives meaning when authentic texts (listening, reading, or viewing) are supported by visuals or when the topic is very familiar. Comprehends texts ranging in length from lists, to phrases, to simple sentences, often with graphically organized information.	Comprehends simple stories, routine correspondence, short descriptive texts or other selections within familiar contexts. Generally comprehends connected sentences and much paragraph-like discourse. Comprehends information-rich texts with highly predictable order.	Comprehends paragraph discourse such as that found in stories, straightforward literary works, personal and work-related correspondence, written reports or instructions, oral presentations (news), anecdotes, descriptive texts, and other texts dealing with topics of a concrete nature.
Language Control	Primarily relies on vocabulary to derive meaning from texts. May derive meaning by recognizing structural patterns that have been used in familiar and some new contexts.	Sufficient control of language (vocabulary, structures, conventions of spoken and written language, etc.) to understand fully and with ease short, non-complex texts on familiar topics; limited control of language to understand some more complex texts. May derive meaning by: • Comparing target language structures with those of the native language • Recognizing parallels in structure between new and familiar language	Sufficient control of language (vocabulary, structures, conventions of spoken and written language, etc.) to understand fully and with ease more complex and descriptive texts with connected language and cohesive devices. Derives meaning by: • Understanding sequencing, time frames, and chronology • Classifying words or concepts according to word order or grammatical use
Vocabulary	Comprehends some, but not all of the time, highly predictable vocabulary, a limited number of words related to familiar topics, and formulaic expressions.	Comprehends high frequency vocabulary related to everyday topics and high frequency idiomatic expressions.	Comprehends generic and some specific vocabulary and structures, specialized and precise vocabulary on topics related to one's experience, and an expanding number of idiomatic expressions.
Communication Strategies	May use some or all of the following strategies to comprehend texts, able to: • Skim and scan • Rely on visual support and background knowledge • Predict meaning based on context, prior knowledge, and/or experience For alphabetic languages: • Rely on recognition of cognates • May recognize word family roots, prefixes, and suffixes	May use some or all of the following strategies to comprehend texts, able to: • Skim and scan • Use visual support and background knowledge • Predict meaning based on context, prior knowledge, and/or experience • Use context clues • Recognize word family roots, prefixes and suffixes For non-alphabetic languages: • Recognize radicals	Comprehends fully the intent of the message, adapting strategies for one's own purposes; uses some or all of the following strategies, able to: • Skim and scan • Use visual support and background knowledge • Predicts meaning based on context, prior knowledge, and/or experience • Use context clues • Use linguistic knowledge • Identify the organizing principle of the text • Create inferences • Differentiate main ideas from supporting details in order to verify
Cultural Awareness	Uses own culture to derive meaning from texts that are heard, read, or viewed.	Generally relies heavily on knowledge of own culture with increasing knowledge of the target culture(s) to interpret texts that are heard, read, or viewed.	Uses knowledge of cultural differences between own culture and target culture(s) as well as increasing knowledge of the target culture(s) to interpret texts that are heard, read, or viewed.

Appendix F | NCSSFL-ACTFL Global Can-Do Benchmarks

	Novice Low	Novice Mid	Novice High	Intermediate Low	Intermediate Mid	Intermediate High
Interpersonal Communication	I can communicate on some very familiar topics using single words and phrases that I have practiced and memorized.	I can communicate on very familiar topics using a variety of words and phrases that I have practiced and memorized.	I can communicate and exchange information about familiar topics using phrases and simple sentences, sometimes supported by memorized language. I can usually handle short social interactions in everyday situations by asking and answering simple questions.	I can participate in conversations on a number of familiar topics using simple sentences. I can handle short social interactions in everyday situations by asking and answering simple questions.	I can participate in conversations on familiar topics using sentences and series of sentences. I can handle short social interactions in everyday situations by asking and answering a variety of questions. I can usually say what I want to say about myself and my everyday life.	I can participate with ease and confidence in conversations on familiar topics. I can usually talk about events and experiences in various time frames. I can usually describe people, places, and things. I can handle social interactions in everyday situations, sometimes even when there is an unexpected complication.
Presentational Speaking	I can present information about myself and some other very familiar topics using single words or memorized phrases.	I can present information about myself and some other very familiar topics using a variety of words, phrases, and memorized expressions.	I can present basic information on familiar topics using language I have practiced using phrases and simple sentences.	I can present information on most familiar topics using a series of simple sentences.	I can make presentations on a wide variety of familiar topics using connected sentences.	I can make presentations in a generally organized way on school, work, and community topics, and on topics I have researched. I can make presentations on some events and experiences in various time frames.
Presentational Writing	I can copy some familiar words, characters, or phrases.	I can write lists and memorized phrases on familiar topics.	I can write short messages and notes on familiar topics related to everyday life.	I can write briefly about most familiar topics and present information using a series of simple sentences.	I can write on a wide variety of familiar topics using connected sentences.	I can write on topics related to school, work, and community in a generally organized way. I can write some simple paragraphs about events and experiences in various time frames.
Interpretive Listening	I can recognize a few memorized words and phrases when I hear them spoken.	I can recognize some familiar words and phrases when I hear them spoken.	I can often understand words, phrases, and simple sentences related to everyday life. I can recognize pieces of information and sometimes understand the main topic of what is being said.	I can understand the main idea in short, simple messages and presentations on familiar topics. I can understand the main idea of simple conversations that I overhear.	I can understand the main idea in messages and presentations on a variety of topics related to everyday life and personal interests and studies. I can understand the main idea in conversations that I overhear.	I can easily understand the main idea in messages and presentations on a variety of topics related to everyday life and personal interests and studies. I can usually understand a few details of what I overhear in conversations, even when something unexpected is expressed. I can sometimes follow what I hear about events and experiences in various time frames.
Interpretive Reading	I can recognize a few letters or characters. I can identify a few memorized words and phrases when I read.	I can recognize some letters or characters. I can understand some learned or memorized words and phrases when I read.	I can understand familiar words, phrases, and sentences within short and simple texts related to everyday life. I can sometimes understand the main idea of what I have read.	I can understand the main idea of short and simple texts when the topic is familiar.	I can understand the main idea of texts related to everyday life and personal interests or studies.	I can easily understand the main idea of texts related to everyday life, personal interests, and studies. I can sometimes follow stories and descriptions about events and experiences in various time frames.

Advanced Low	Advanced Mid	Advanced High	Superior	Distinguished	
I can participate in conversations about familiar topics that go beyond my everyday life. I can talk in an organized way and with some detail about events and experiences in various time frames. I can describe people, places, and things in an organized way and with some detail. I can handle a familiar situation with an unexpected complication.	I can express myself fully not only on familiar topics but also on some concrete social, academic, and professional topics. I can talk in detail and in an organized way about events and experiences in various time frames. I can confidently handle routine situations with an unexpected complication. I can share my point of view in discussions on some complex issues.	I can express myself freely and spontaneously, and for the most part accurately, on concrete topics and on most complex issues. I can usually support my opinion and develop hypotheses on topics of particular interest or personal expertise.	I can communicate with ease, accuracy, and fluency. I can participate fully and effectively in discussions on a variety of topics in formal and informal settings. I can discuss at length complex issues by structuring arguments and developing hypotheses.	I can communicate reflectively on a wide range of global issues and highly abstract concepts in a culturally sophisticated manner.	**Interpersonal Communication**
I can deliver organized presentations appropriate to my audience on a variety of topics. I can present information about events and experiences in various time frames.	I can deliver well-organized presentations on concrete social, academic, and professional topics. I can present detailed information about events and experiences in various time frames.	I can deliver detailed presentations, usually with accuracy, clarity and precision, on a variety of topics and issues related to community interests and some special fields of expertise.	I can deliver detailed presentations with accuracy, clarity, and precision to a wide variety of audiences on topics and issues ranging from broad general interests to areas of specialized expertise.	I can deliver sophisticated and articulate presentations on a wide range of global issues and highly abstract concepts in a culturally appropriate manner, tailored to a variety of audiences.	**Presentational Speaking**
I can write on general interest, academic, and professional topics. I can write organized paragraphs about events and experiences in various time frames.	I can write on a wide variety of general interest, professional, and academic topics. I can write well-organized, detailed paragraphs in various time frames.	I can write extensively with significant precision and detail on a variety of topics, most complex issues, and some special fields of expertise.	I can write about complex and abstract issues ranging from topics of broad general interests to areas of specialized expertise using standard structure, lexicon, and writing protocols.	I can write about global issues from highly conceptualized and analytical perspectives. I can tailor my writing to sophisticated readers.	**Presentational Writing**
I can understand the main idea and some supporting details in organized speech on a variety of topics of personal and general interest. I can follow stories and descriptions of some length and in various time frames. I can understand information presented in a variety of genres on familiar topics, even when something unexpected is expressed.	I can understand the main idea and most supporting details on a variety of topics of personal and general interest, as well as some topics of professional interest. I can follow stories and descriptions of some length and in various time frames. I can understand information presented in most genres, even when not familiar with the topic.	I can easily follow narrative, informational, and descriptive speech. I can understand discussions on most topics that deal with special interests, unfamiliar situations, and abstract concepts. I can sometimes follow extended arguments and different points of view.	I can follow a wide range of academic and professional discourse on abstract and specialized topics. I can understand all standard dialects. I can sometimes infer complex meaning that requires deep understanding of the culture.	I can understand highly abstract and specialized speech tailored to different audiences. I can understand sophisticated language, humor, and persuasive arguments embedded with cultural references and allusions.	**Interpretive Listening**
I can understand the main idea and some supporting details on a variety of topics of personal and general interest. I can follow stories and descriptions of some length and in various time frames and genres.	I can understand the main idea and most supporting details in texts on a variety of topics of personal and general interest, as well as some professional topics. I can follow stories and descriptions of considerable length and in various time frames. I can understand texts written in a variety of genres, even when I am unfamiliar with the topic.	I can easily follow narrative, informational, and descriptive texts. I can understand what I read on most topics that deal with special interests, unfamiliar situations, and abstract concepts. I can sometimes understand extended arguments and different points of view.	I can follow academic, professional, and literary texts on a wide range of both familiar and unfamiliar subjects. I can sometimes infer complex meaning that requires analysis and deep understanding of the culture.	I can understand with ease and confidence highly abstract and specialized texts that are succinct or elaborate. I can follow unpredictable turns of thought. I can manage inference from within the cultural framework.	**Interpretive Reading**

Appendix G | Essential Questions

	Novice	→	Intermediate	→	Advanced
Belonging	What is a family?	→	What is friendship?	→	Why is global collaboration important?
	How do I contribute to my community?		How do people, places, and events define a community?		How do communities remain vital?
Challenges	What are the rights of a child?	→	Why can't all children go to school?	→	Why is lifelong learning a necessity in the 21st century?
	What is hunger?		What is the connection between clean water and quality of life?		How does overpopulation impact quality of life around the world?
Creativity	How do I contribute to society?	→	How do you use your imagination?	→	How can schools encourage creativity and innovation?
	What do artists do?		How do music and art reflect society?		What makes a piece of literature a classic?
Discovery	Who are the inventors?	→	How are advances in science impacting my life today?	→	What inventions are needed to improve the quality of life on earth?
	Who are the explorers?		What parts of our world need to be explored?		Where are the next frontiers to explore?
Exploring Time and Place	What dates are important on my personal timeline?	→	What events from (France's) past continue to influence (France) today?	→	Why do people say that history repeats itself?
	What makes a city special?		How does where I live influence my lifestyle?		Why do people say: It's a great place to visit, but I wouldn't want to live there?
Identity	Who am I?	→	How do family and friends influence who I am?	→	How does learning another language and culture influence who I am and my view of the world?
	How does what I do define who I am?		What am I doing to gain the skills that I am likely to need for my future?		How is my identity shaped over time?
Well-Being	How do people here and in (the French-speaking world) describe a balanced lifestyle?	→	What impact does technology have on our lifestyles?	→	What role does media play in shaping public opinion?
	Where does our food come from?		Eat to live or live to eat: What is the difference?		Why consider joining the "slow food" movement?

Appendix H | Balanced Lifestyle Unit

Language and Level/Grade:	French – Novice Mid ➔ Novice High	Approximate Length:	6 weeks
		Approximate Number of Minutes Weekly:	250 minutes

Theme/Topic	Well-Being: A Balanced Lifestyle
Essential Question	How do people here and in (the French-speaking world) describe a balanced lifestyle?

Goals *What should learners know and be able to do by the end of the unit?*	Learners will be able to: • Explore health and wellness websites to identify elements of a balanced lifestyle here and in (country). • Compare lifestyles of teenagers to teenagers in (country) in terms of balance. • Make recommendations for ways to create or maintain a balanced lifestyle. • Create a presentation for (the community) highlighting ways to encourage a balanced lifestyle.

Summative Performance Assessment • *These tasks allow learners to demonstrate how well they have met the goals of the unit.* • *They are integrated throughout the unit.* • *The template encourages multiple interpretive tasks.* • *The interpretive tasks inform the content of the presentational and interpersonal tasks.* • *The tasks should incorporate 21st Century Skills.*	**Interpretive Mode**		
	Learners will read a blog written by a teenager where he discusses his activities. They will demonstrate comprehension by answering questions about main ideas and will complete a graphic organizer based on information found in the text.	Learners will watch a commercial for a product that promises to make life easier or less stressful and will demonstrate comprehension by analyzing the effectiveness of the message and product.	Learners will read a schedule of a top athlete to determine how he spends the hours in his day deciding what elements are part of a balanced lifestyle and what is missing.
	Presentational Mode Learners will create a presentation based on multiple sources of information highlighting ways to promote a balanced lifestyle for teenagers. The presentation will be shared with another French class.	**Interpersonal Mode** In pairs or small groups, learners share what they have learned about their lifestyle and the lifestyle of teenagers in (France) in terms of a balanced lifestyle. They compare their daily routines and schedules and make and respond to suggestions to adjust their lifestyle.	

Cultures (Sample Evidence) *Indicate the relationship between the product, practice, and perspective.*	**Product:** Café **Practice:** Stopping with friends for coffee **Perspective:** It's not the coffee, it's the conversation. **Product:** School year calendar **Practice:** Regular breaks, holidays **Perspective:** Balance

Connections (Sample Evidence)	**Making Connections**	**Acquiring Information and Diverse Perspectives**
	Health and wellness: • Compare recommendations for healthy lifestyles. **Media studies:** • Consider impact of media on lifestyle considerations like diet and exercise.	Importance of vacation and family time Tradition of *"Fermature annuelle"* (annual closing) in France Differences in school schedules

Comparisons (Sample Evidence)	**Language Comparisons**	**Cultural Comparisons**
	• *la joie de vivre* (joy of living) • *métro, boulot, dodo* (subway, work, sleep) • *Ne t'en fais pas!* (Don't worry!) • *la détente* (relaxation) • Making polite recommendations	• Work time/leisure time • Mealtime with/without family • Weekend activities • Walking/driving • Teenagers working during school year/summer • Life expectancies

Communities (Sample Evidence)	School and Global Communities	Lifelong Learning
	Share information on wellness with community.	Examine personal lifestyle and make adjustments as needed.

Connections to Common Core	
	Reading: 1. Read closely to determine what the text says explicitly and to make logical inferences from it; cite specific textual evidence when writing or speaking to support conclusions drawn from the text. **Writing: 6.** Use technology, including the Internet, to produce and publish writing and to interact and collaborate with others. **Writing: 7.** Conduct short as well as more sustained research projects based on focused questions, demonstrating understanding of the subject under investigation. **Speaking and Listening: 1.** Prepare for and participate effectively in a range of conversations and collaborations with diverse partners, building on others' ideas and expressing their own clearly and persuasively. **Language: 4.** Determine or clarify the meaning of unknown and multiple-meaning words and phrases by using context clues, analyzing meaningful word parts, and consulting general and specialized reference materials, as appropriate.

Toolbox

Language Functions	Related Structures/Patterns	Vocabulary Expansion
		Tier 1
Compare lifestyle routines	*plus que, moins que, aussi que* (more than, less than, as…as)	sports, activities expressions/adverbs of frequency
Describe your daily schedule	*(le) lundi…* (on Mondays)	**Tier 2**
Ask and answer questions about daily routines	interrogative pronouns and adjectives	*Une bonne hygiène de vie* (a healthy lifestyle)
Express frequency, saying when and how often you do certain things	adverbs	*Un régime équilibré* (a balanced diet) *La détente* (relaxation)
Express needs, saying what you need to do to be healthy	*Il faut/Il me faut* (It's necessary/I need)	*s'entraîner* (to exercise) *se détendre/se dépêcher* (to relax/to hurry)
Express opinions about daily activities, schedules	*Il est important de, Il est bon de* (It's important to/it's good to)	*Être détendu/être stressé* (to be relaxed/to be stressed)
Make suggestions about ways to be healthy	*Tu devrais/Vous devriez* *Il te/vous faut* (You should/you need to)	

Key Learning Activities/Formative Assessments			
Key Learning Activity/ Formative Assessment *(representative samples from beginning to end of unit)*	**How does this activity support the unit goals or performance tasks?**	**Mode of Communication**	**Interculturality** **S**elf **C**ommunity **W**orld
Read article on how French teenagers spend free time. Design survey questions to use with learners studying French. Create graphic organizer to compare school results to those in article. Discuss results in groups.	how French teens spend free time and make comparisons	Interpretive Presentational Interpersonal	C, W
Work in groups to create a multimedia presentation that explains *métro, boulot, dodo* (subway, work, sleep) in the context of a teenager's life in the United States.	product that explains the lifestyle of a U.S. teenager to French teens	Interpersonal Presentational	C, W
Watch silent movie—UNICEF clip on right of child to play. Discuss and compare to *metro, boulot, dodo* (subway, work, sleep) presentations.	concept of balanced lifestyle from different perspective	Interpretive Interpersonal	C, W
Read *French Girl in Seattle: Une Visite au café* (A visit to the café). Select an image from the article or a personal image. Explain the role of the café from the perspective of the article and from your perspective. Post your image and comments.	introduce learners to cafés; allows learners to process concept of café	Presentational Interpersonal	S, C
Read article *Les lycéens se retrouvent au café* (High school students meet in the café); discuss what you like and don't like about the activities; consider what the equivalent might be in your community.	consider role of café for teens and make comparisons	Interpretive Interpersonal	S, C
Compare two *Maisons des Jeunes* (youth recreation centers) for hours and activities. Compare to local recreational facility.	importance of teen centers and comparison to U.S.	Interpretive	S, C, W
Create a proposal for a local teen café or an advertisement for one that already exists.	determine needs of local community and address those needs	Presentational	S, C
Read article on importance of sleep; discuss typical sleep habits.	summarize healthy behaviors; give advice; served as model of how they might present	Interpretive Presentational	S
View video *La moitié des ados manquent de sommeil* (Half of teenagers lack sleep).	listen for specific issues/ advice	Interpretive	S, W
Select an article from the website mangerbouger.fr that deals with health and wellness. Read individually first. Then, identify key points with group. Decide how to best share information with other groups.	initial preparation for possible wellness fair presentations	Interpretive Presentational Interpersonal	S, C, W

Resources	Technology Integration
Text for Interpretive Tasks: • www3.sympatico.ca/serge.richard2/ • www3.sympatico.ca/serge.richard2/page5.html Additional resources available at: • www.actfl.org/publications/books-and-brochures/the-keys-planning-learning	Teachers can create a safe, free space for learner blogs and more: • kidblog.org

Appendix I | Blank Unit Template

Language and Level/Grade:		Approximate Length:	
		Approximate Number of Minutes Weekly:	
Theme/Topic			
Essential Question			
Goals *What should learners know and be able to do by the end of the unit?*			

| **Summative Performance Assessment** • *These tasks allow learners to demonstrate how well they have met the goals of the unit.* • *They are integrated throughout the unit.* • *The template encourages multiple interpretive tasks.* • *The interpretive tasks inform the content of the presentational and interpersonal tasks.* • *The tasks should incorporate 21st Century Skills.* | **Interpretive Mode** | | |
| | **Presentational Mode** | **Interpersonal Mode** | |

Cultures (Sample Evidence) *Indicate the relationship between the product, practice, and perspective.*	Product: Practice: Perspective: Product: Practice: Perspective:		
Connections (Sample Evidence)	**Making Connections**	**Acquiring Information and Diverse Perspectives**	
Comparisons (Sample Evidence)	**Language Comparisons**	**Cultural Comparisons**	
Communities (Sample Evidence)	**School and Global Communities**	**Lifelong Learning**	
Connections to Common Core			

Toolbox		
Language Functions	**Related Structures/Patterns**	**Vocabulary Expansion**
		Tier 1
		Tier 2

Key Learning Activities/Formative Assessments			
Key Learning Activity/ Formative Assessment *(representative samples from beginning to end of unit)*	**How does this activity support the unit goals or performance tasks?**	**Mode of Communication**	**Interculturality** **S**elf **C**ommunity **W**orld

Resources	Technology Integration

Appendix J | Common Core Anchor Standards

Reading

Key Ideas and Details

R1: Read closely to determine what the text says explicitly and to make logical inferences from it; cite specific textual evidence when writing or speaking to support conclusions drawn from the text.

R2: Determine central ideas or themes of a text and analyze their development; summarize the key supporting details and ideas.

R3: Analyze how and why individuals, events, and ideas develop and interact over the course of a text.

Craft and Structure

R4: Interpret words and phrases as they are used in a text, including determining technical, connotative, and figurative meanings, and analyze how specific word choices shape meaning or tone.

R5: Analyze the structure of texts, including how specific sentences, paragraphs, and larger portions of the text (e.g., a section, chapter, scene, or stanza) relate to each other and the whole.

R6: Assess how point of view or purpose shapes the content and style of a text.

Integration of Knowledge and Ideas

R7: Integrate and evaluate content presented in diverse formats and media, including visually and quantitatively, as well as in words.

R8: Delineate and evaluate the argument and specific claims in a text, including the validity of the reasoning as well as the relevance and sufficiency of the evidence.

R9: Analyze how two or more texts address similar themes or topics in order to build knowledge or to compare the approaches the authors take.

Range of Reading and Level of Text Complexity

R10: Read and comprehend complex literary and informational texts independently and proficiently.

Writing

Text Types and Purposes

W1: Write arguments to support claims in an analysis of substantive topics or texts, using valid reasoning and relevant and sufficient evidence.

W2: Write informative/explanatory texts to examine and convey complex ideas and information clearly and accurately through the effective selection, organization, and analysis of content.

W3: Write narratives to develop real or imagined experiences or events using effective technique, well-chosen details, and well-structured event sequences.

Production and Distribution of Writing

W4: Produce clear and coherent writing in which the development, organization, and style are appropriate to task, purpose, and audience.

W5: Develop and strengthen writing as needed by planning, revising, editing, rewriting, or trying a new approach.

W6: Use technology, including the Internet, to produce and publish writing and to interact and collaborate with others.

Research to Build and Present Knowledge

W7: Conduct short as well as more sustained research projects based on focused questions, demonstrating understanding of the subject under investigation.

W8: Gather relevant information from multiple print and digital sources, assess the credibility and accuracy of each source, and integrate the information while avoiding plagiarism.

W9: Draw evidence from literary or informational texts to support analysis, reflection, and research.

Range of Writing

W10: Write routinely over extended time frames (time for research, reflection, and revision) and shorter time frames (a single sitting or a day or two) for a range of tasks, purposes, and audiences.

Speaking and Listening

Comprehension and Collaboration

SL1: Prepare for and participate effectively in a range of conversations and collaborations with diverse partners, building on others' ideas, and expressing their own clearly and persuasively.

SL2: Integrate and evaluate information presented in diverse media and formats, including visually, quantitatively, and orally.

SL3: Evaluate a speaker's point of view, reasoning, and use of evidence and rhetoric.

Presentation of Knowledge and Ideas

SL4: Present information, findings, and supporting evidence such that listeners can follow the line of reasoning and the organization, development, and style are appropriate to task, purpose, and audience.

SL5: Make strategic use of digital media and visual displays of data to express information and enhance understanding of presentations.

SL6: Adapt speech to a variety of contexts and communicative tasks, demonstrating command of formal English when indicated or appropriate.

Language

Conventions of Standard English

L1: Demonstrate command of the conventions of standard English grammar and usage when writing or speaking.

L2: Demonstrate command of the conventions of standard English capitalization, punctuation, and spelling when writing.

Knowledge of Language

L3: Apply knowledge of language to understand how language functions in different contexts, to make effective choices for meaning or style, and to comprehend more fully when reading or listening.

Vocabulary Acquisition and Use

L4: Determine or clarify the meaning of unknown and multiple-meaning words and phrases by using context clues, analyzing meaningful word parts, and consulting general and specialized reference materials, as appropriate.

L5: Demonstrate understanding of figurative language, word relationships, and nuances in word meanings.

L6: Acquire and use accurately a range of general academic and domain-specific words and phrases sufficient for reading, writing, speaking, and listening at the college and career readiness level; demonstrate independence in gathering vocabulary knowledge when considering a word or phrase important to comprehension or expression.

Appendix K | Language Functions

Accepting/refusing invitations

Agreeing/disagreeing

Analyzing/interpreting

Apologizing/forgiving

Approving/disapproving

Asking for/giving clarification

Asking for/giving information

Asking for/giving/refusing permission

Attracting attention

Blaming

Clarifying

Comparing/contrasting

Complaining

Complimenting

Confirming/admitting/denying

Congratulating

Contradicting

Counting

Defining

Describing events

Describing people

Describing places

Describing procedures, processes

Describing objects

Describing weather

Discussing

Encouraging

Evaluating

Explaining

Expressing cause and effect

Expressing certainty/uncertainty

Expressing comprehension or lack of comprehension

Expressing daily routines

Expressing doubt/indecision

Expressing emotions, feelings

Expressing hope

Expressing how often, how well

Expressing intentions

Expressing interest/lack of interest/ indifference or boredom

Expressing likes/dislikes/preferences

Expressing needs/wishes/wants

Expressing obligation

Expressing opinions

Expressing possibility/impossibility

Expressing probability/improbability

Expressing regret

Expressing surprise

Expressing sympathy

Extending invitations

Giving advice

Giving biographical information (name, address, phone number, age)

Giving commands

Giving directions

Giving possible solutions

Giving reasons and explaining causality

Greeting/welcoming

Hypothesizing

Identifying

Identifying day, date, season

Indicating relationships

Instructing

Introducing oneself/someone else

Justifying

Leave-taking/farewells

Listing

Maintaining a conversation

Making appointments, arrangements, reservations

Making recommendations

Mediating or conciliating

Narrating

Negotiating

Offering

Offering alternatives/solutions

Opening/closing an interaction

Persuading/dissuading

Planning

Praising/blaming

Presenting information

Promising

Recounting experiences/events

Referring to things already mentioned

Reporting

Requesting

Responding

Seeking/requesting information

Sequencing

Speculating on the future

Stating location

Stating ownership

Suggesting

Summarizing

Talking about the future

Telling time

Telling/Retelling stories

Thanking

Turn taking (conversational)

Using formal/informal language appropriately

Warning

Appendix L | Balanced Lifestyle Lesson Plan

Language Level: Novice Mid - High	Grade: 9–12	Date: xx	Day in Unit: 2	Minutes: 55

Unit Theme and Question	**Contemporary Life:** A Balanced Lifestyle *How do people here and in (the French-speaking world) describe a balanced lifestyle?*

Daily Topic:	*métro, boulot, dodo* (subway, work, sleep)

STANDARDS	LESSON OBJECTIVES		
What are the communicative and cultural objectives for the lesson?	**Communication and Cultures**	*Which modes of communication will be addressed?* ✔ Interpersonal ✔ Interpretive ☐ Presentational	**Learners can:** Name obligations and activities that create balance in daily life based on authentic video *Ma Vie au Soleil* (My Life in the Sun) Ask and answer questions about what they do to create balance in their lives
If applicable, indicate how Connections/Comparisons/ Communities/Common Core will be part of your lesson.	**Connections**		
	Comparisons	Language: *métro, boulot, dodo* (subway, work, sleep)	
	Communities		
	Common Core	**Speaking and Listening: 1**. Prepare for and participate effectively in a range of conversations and collaborations with diverse partners, building on others' ideas and expressing their own clearly and persuasively.	

Lesson Sequence	Activity/Activities What will learners do? What does the teacher do?	Time* How many minutes will this segment take?	Materials → Resources → Technology Be specific. What materials will you develop? What materials will you bring in from other sources?
Gain Attention/ Activate Prior Knowledge	• Teacher displays a variety of images depicting wellness and stress • Learners list activities that they consider to be chores or obligations as well as those that are done by choice or are of interest.	5	• Images depicting wellness/stress • Images of various activities, preferably images that learners have used in previous units
Provide Input	• Learners are given a set of statements concerning the video content. • The teacher reads each statement, taking time to develop comprehension. • Learners are asked if they agree or disagree with the statements. • Learners will be asked to find proof for or against each statement as they work with the video. The video is shown first with no sound. Learners have time to individually note proof for and against based on visual images. • Learners also list any words that they expect to hear in the video.	10	• Video *Ma Vie au Soleil* • Proof for/proof against activity page.

Elicit Performance/ Provide Feedback	• Learners indicate by signaling thumbs up or down if they have proof for or against each statement after watching the video. • They pair to share their comments on proof for/proof against statements. They compare their ideas with their partner's and each adds details to their individual lists. • The teacher asks two or three "non-volunteers" to share their responses and then calls on volunteers. • The teacher then asks learners to share words or phrases that they anticipate hearing in the video based on what they saw.	10	
Provide Input	• The teacher introduces the concept of *métro, boulot, dodo*. • Learners watch the video for a second time with sound on, identifying words on their lists that connect to the concept of going to work or working. • The teacher shares a prepared list of activities drawing from those in the video and from those suggested by learners during the warm-up. Learners review and learn new sentence and question frames—What do you do? I do/don't…Do you like…? I like/don't like, Do you want? I want/don't want, Do you have to…? I have to/don't have to—while working with the list of activities.	10	• Images depicting *métro, boulot, dodo* • Prepared list of activities based on video
Elicit Performance/ Provide Feedback	• Learners work individually to complete a graphic organizer writing simple sentences about things they do that relate to the routine of work and things they do for fun. • Learners pair and rotate in inner–outer circles to see what they have in common.	10	• Graphic organizer—work, fun and overlap for both
Closure	• Learners are given an image of *métro, boulot, dodo*. They write down any words or sentences that they associate with the images. These are collected and may be used as future prompts for discussion.	5	• Image representative of *métro, boulot, dodo*
Enhance Retention & Transfer	• Consider the balance in your life. Take the online quiz—Test your stress smarts. Consider how you might comment on your results in French in class. • fit.webmd.com/kids/mood/rmq/rm-quiz-kids-stress-test • Alternatively, read part of the online article about health and well-being of teens around the world. Consider how you might share some of what you learned in French in class. (mchb.hrsa.gov/mchirc/_pubs/us_teens/main_pages/ch_1.htm)		• Articles or references in English or French to enhance awareness of the importance of a balanced lifestyle
Reflection—Notes to Self	• What worked well? Why? • What didn't work? Why? • What changes would you make if you taught this lesson again?		

* Remember that the maximum attention span of the learner is approximately the age of the learner up to 20 minutes. The initial lesson cycle (gain attention/activate prior knowledge, provide input, and elicit performance/provide feedback) should not take more than 20 minutes. The second cycle (provide input and elicit performance/provide feedback) should be repeated as needed and will vary depending on the length of the class period.

Appendix M | Blank Lesson Plan Template

Language Level:	Grade:	Date:	Day in Unit:	Minutes:

Unit Theme and Question	
Daily Topic:	

STANDARDS	LESSON OBJECTIVES		
What are the communicative and cultural objectives for the lesson?	**Communication and Cultures**	*Which modes of communication will be addressed?* ☐ Interpersonal ☐ Interpretive ☐ Presentational	**Students can:**
If applicable, indicate how Connections/Comparisons/ Communities/Common Core will be part of your lesson.	**Connections**		
	Comparisons		
	Communities		
	Common Core		

Lesson Sequence	Activity/Activities What will learners do? What does the teacher do?	Time* How many minutes will this segment take?	Materials → Resources → Technology Be specific. What materials will you develop? What materials will you bring in from other sources?
Gain Attention/ Activate Prior Knowledge			
Provide Input			
Elicit Performance/ Provide Feedback			

Provide Input	• If applicable		
Elicit Performance/ Provide Feedback	• If applicable		
Closure			
Enhance Retention & Transfer			
Reflection—Notes to Self	• What worked well? Why? • What didn't work? Why? • What changes would you make if you taught this lesson again?		

* Remember that the maximum attention span of the learner is approximately the age of the learner up to 20 minutes. The initial lesson cycle (gain attention/activate prior knowledge, provide input, and elicit performance/provide feedback) should not take more than 20 minutes. The second cycle (provide input and elicit performance/provide feedback) should be repeated as needed and will vary depending on the length of the class period.

Appendix N | Chinese Lesson Plan for Third Grade

Language Level: Novice	Grade: 3	Date: xx	Day in Unit: xx	Minutes: 25

Unit Theme and Question	**Families and Communities:** *How does where I live influence what I eat?*
Daily Topic:	Agriculture in China's 5 regions

STANDARDS	LESSON OBJECTIVES		
What are the communicative and cultural objectives for the lesson?	**Communication and Cultures**	*Which modes of communication will be addressed?* ✔ Interpersonal ☐ Interpretive ☐ Presentational	**Learners can:** Identify agricultural products of the five regions of China.
If applicable, indicate how Connections/Comparisons/Communities/Common Core will be part of your lesson.	**Connections**	Associate geography with agricultural products	
	Comparisons		
	Communities		
	Common Core	**Speaking and Listening: 1.** Prepare for and participate effectively in a range of conversations and collaborations with diverse partners, building on others' ideas and expressing their own clearly and persuasively.	

Lesson Sequence	Activity/Activities What will learners do? What does the teacher do?	Time* How many minutes will this segment take?	Materials → Resources → Technology Be specific. What materials will you develop? What materials will you bring in from other sources?
Gain Attention/ Activate Prior Knowledge	• Teachers share geography visuals. • Learners will work in small groups to place geography visuals on the map of China. • After completing this activity, learners will take turns placing large velcro visuals on a shower curtain map of China so that everyone can check their group maps for accuracy.	5	• Shower curtain map of China • Velcro images of geography of different regions of China • Blank maps of China for learner groups • Envelopes of geography images to accompany blank maps of China
Provide Input	• Learners will repeat the names of agricultural products as the teacher shows them to the class.	3	• Images of corn, wheat, chicken, cattle, lamb, soybean, duck
Elicit Performance/ Provide Feedback	• Learners will move to five different stations around the room, identify the region and the geographic features of the region (review), and learn the agricultural products associated with the region. • After learners move to a new station, they identify the region and geographic feature, learn the agricultural products associated with the new region. • The teacher makes simple comparisons between regions: Does the (north) have (chicken)? What region has (chicken)?	15	• Five stations with visuals of the geography of the region and map of China showing the region • Visuals of agricultural products
Provide Input	• *if applicable*		
Elicit Performance/ Provide Feedback	• *if applicable*		

Closure	• Learners return to their groups and maps of China. They place agricultural products on the maps. • After completing this activity, learners take turns placing large velcro visuals on a shower curtain map of China so that everyone can check their group maps for accuracy. The teacher asks: What region has (chicken)?	7	• Shower curtain map of China • Velcro images of agricultural products • Blank maps of China for groups • Envelopes of agricultural products for groups
Enhance Retention & Transfer			
Reflection—Notes to Self	• What worked well? Why? • What didn't work? Why? • What changes would you make if you taught this lesson again?		

* Remember that the maximum attention span of the learner is approximately the age of the learner up to 20 minutes. The initial lesson cycle (gain attention/activate prior knowledge, provide input and elicit performance/provide feedback) should not take more than 20 minutes. The second cycle (provide input and elicit performance/provide feedback) should be repeated as needed and will vary depending on the length of the class period.

Glossary

Authentic Tasks: An authentic task is one which requires the student to use knowledge or skills to produce a product or complete a performance that is useful beyond the classroom.

Authentic Texts: Those written and oral communications produced by members of a language and culture group for members of the same language and culture group (Shrum & Glisan, 2010, p. 85).

Backward Design: The teacher starts with desired outcomes and acceptable evidence and then plans appropriate learning activities to reach those outcomes (Wiggins & McTighe, 2005).

Bloom's Taxonomy of Thinking: Classification of learning objectives created by Benjamin S. Bloom and colleagues in 1956. It was updated in 2000 by Loren Anderson, a former student of Bloom. The updated taxonomy moves from lower order to higher order thinking skills: Remember, Understand, Apply, Analyze, Evaluate, Create.

Brain-Based Learning: Those practices that are compatible with what we know about how the brain learns.

Can-Do Statements: Based on the ACTFL Proficiency Guidelines, Can-Do Statements tell what language learners can understand and communicate in the language(s) they are learning.

Circumlocution: The use of language that one does know in order to explain a specific word that one does not know (ACTFL 2012 Proficiency Guidelines Glossary).

Code-Switching: Switching from one language to another to complete an idea, thought, or sentence, often when one lacks the word or phrase in the language one started off in (ACTFL 2012 Proficiency Guidelines Glossary).

Cognates: Words between languages that have a common origin and are therefore readily understood. For example, the French word "leçon" and the English word "lesson" (ACTFL 2012 Proficiency Guidelines Glossary).

Cohesive Devices: Language components that link ideas for smooth flow within and among sentences and paragraphs, such as conjunctions, relative pronouns, pronoun substitutions (subject, verb), adverbs of time, and subordinate clauses (ACTFL 2012 Proficiency Guidelines Glossary).

Common Core State Standards: The Common Core State Standards Initiative is a state-led effort that established a single set of clear educational standards for kindergarten through 12th grade in English language arts and mathematics that states voluntarily adopt. The standards are designed to ensure that students graduating from high school are prepared to enter credit bearing entry courses in two or four year college programs or enter the workforce (www.corestandards.org).

Communication Strategies: How the language learner makes himself understood (repeating, paraphrasing, etc.) and what he does to understand others (e.g., asks for repetition, slowing of speech).

Comprehensible Input: The amount of language a learner can fully understand plus a little more, i + 1 (Krashen, 1982).

Content: Topics that the learner can understand and discuss.

Context: Situation within which the language learner understands and communicates.

Cultural Awareness: How the language learner uses knowledge of the target culture to understand and communicate in the target language.

Culture Triangle: The relationship of cultural products and practices to the underlying perspectives of a people.

Curriculum: Curriculum includes the knowledge and skills that successful students are expected to learn, organized to plan learning. In the case of world language instruction, the curriculum is based on the Proficiency Guidelines that describe the pathway to increased understanding and communication in the target language.

Differentiation: The process of providing students with different ways of presenting concepts and ideas so that all students can learn regardless of their abilities.

Discourse: Communication of ideas or information through speech or writing.

Domains of Performance: Describe the language learners' performance in terms of functions, contexts, text type, language control, vocabulary, communication strategies, and cultural awareness.

Enduring Understanding: Statements summarizing important ideas that are central to a discipline and have lasting value beyond the classroom.

Essential Questions: "Questions that are not answerable with finality in a brief sentence . . . Their aim is to stimulate thought, to provoke inquiry, and to spark more questions—including thoughtful student questions—not just pat answers" (Wiggins & McTighe, 2005, p. 106).

European Language Portfolio: The ELP is a document in which those who are learning or have learned a language—whether at school or outside school—can record and reflect on their language learning and cultural experiences. It is a project of the Council of Europe.

Feedback: Information communicated to the student about performance in order to improve learning.

Fluency: The flow in spoken or written language as perceived by the listener or reader. Flow is made possible by clarity of expression, the acceptable ordering of ideas, and use of vocabulary and syntax appropriate to the context (ACTFL 2012 Proficiency Guidelines Glossary).

Formative Assessment: Monitoring student learning during instruction and providing ongoing feedback to improve learning.

Formulaic: Constituting or containing a verbal formula or set form of words such as "How are you?/Fine, thank you." "Thanks very much./You're welcome." (ACTFL 2012 Proficiency Guidelines Glossary).

Functions: Communicative tasks that a learner can complete in the target language.

Genre: Any category of art, music, film, literature, etc., based on a set of stylistic criteria (ACTFL 2012 Proficiency Guidelines Glossary).

Interculturality: The interaction of people from different cultural backgrounds using authentic language appropriately in a way that demonstrates knowledge and understanding of the cultures. It is the ability to experience the culture of another person and to be open-minded, interested, and curious about that person and culture (www.learnnc.org/lp/editions/linguafolio/6122).

Interpersonal Communication: Two-way exchange of information, ideas, and opinions, both oral and written, that is unrehearsed and requires negotiation of meaning.

Interpretive Communication: Listening, reading, or viewing a message. It is one-way communication without the opportunity for clarification or rephrasing.

Instructional Repertoire: The learning strategies and theories that facilitate instruction in the world language classroom.

Learner-Centered Instruction (or student-centered learning, or student-centered instruction or learner-centered teaching): Student-centered learning (SCL), or learner-centeredness, is a learning model that places the student (learner) in the center of the learning process. In student-centered learning, students are active participants in their learning; they learn at their own pace and use their own strategies; they are more intrinsically than extrinsically motivated; learning is more individualized than standardized. Student-centered learning develops learning-how-to-learn skills such as problem solving, critical thinking, and reflective thinking. Student-centered learning accounts for and adapts to different learning styles of students (National Center for Research on Teacher Learning, 1999) (www.intime.uni.edu/model/center_of_learning_files/definition.html).

Lexical: Of or relating to the words or the vocabulary of a language as distinguished from its grammar and structure (ACTFL 2012 Proficiency Guidelines Glossary).

LinguaFolio®: LinguaFolio® is a formative assessment tool to help language learners self-assess their progress in learning languages. LinguaFolio was developed by members of the National Council of State Supervisors for Languages and is the result of a transatlantic dialogue (sponsored by the Goethe-Institut) among members of the Council of Europe, delegates from the European Ministries of Education, and representatives from state departments of education in the United States.

Literacy: The National Council of Teachers of English (2013) has expanded the traditional definition of literacy (ability to read and write), stating that active, successful participants in this 21st century global society must be able to develop proficiency and fluency with the tools of technology; build intentional cross-cultural connections and relationships with others so to pose and solve problems collaboratively and strengthen independent thought; design and share information for global communities to meet a variety of purposes; manage, analyze, and synthesize multiple streams of simultaneous information; create, critique, analyze, and evaluate multimedia texts; and attend to the ethical responsibilities required by these complex environments.

Mode: A manner of communicating; the National Standards specify three modes of communication: interpersonal, interpretive, and presentational.

Multiple Intelligences: An intelligence is a capacity to process information in certain ways. Each intelligence can be activated in an appropriate cultural setting (Shrum & Glisan, 2010, p. 351).

Narrative: The relating of a story or account of events, experiences, etc., whether true or fictitious, told in a logical and chronological order (ACTFL 2012 Proficiency Guidelines Glossary).

Non-Negotiables: Criteria for a project or assignment that must be met before the project or assignment can be submitted for evaluation.

On-Demand Writing: Writing that is completed during a set period of time without feedback or other outside assistance.

Pacing: The amount of time within a lesson spent on each part of the lesson.

Paragraph: A self-contained, cohesive unit of spoken or written discourse that generally consists of multiple sentences linked by internal organization and connectors (ACTFL 2012 Proficiency Guidelines Glossary).

Paraphrase: Restating the meaning of something spoken or written in one's own words.

Presentational Communication: Polished speaking or writing for an audience. The writer or speaker benefits from rehearsals, feedback, and editing in preparation of the message.

Proficiency: What individuals can do with language in terms of speaking, writing, listening, and reading in real-world situations in a spontaneous, non-rehearsed context (ACTFL 2012 Proficiency Guidelines).

Range of Performance: Descriptors of what the language learner can do at the Novice, Intermediate, and Advanced levels.

Rubric: A document that describes criteria for a project or assignment with levels of quality from "excellent" to "needs more work."

Scaffolding: Providing assistance to the learner to accomplish a task, making it easier for the learner to succeed.

Scoring Guide: A document that lists the expectations for a project or assignment along with indicators showing that the expectation was fully met, partially met, not met.

Specialized Vocabulary: Words, expressions, technical terms, etc., that are meaningful to members of a specific group or field of study or endeavor (ACTFL 2012 Proficiency Guidelines Glossary).

Strings of Sentences: A series of isolated or discrete sentences typically referring to a given topic but not grammatically or syntactically connected (ACTFL 2012 Proficiency Guidelines Glossary).

Summative Assessment: Used to evaluate student learning at the end of a unit or semester or course.

Target Language: The language other than one's native language that is being learned.

Text Type: Words, phrases, sentences, strings of sentences, or paragraphs.

Theme: A unifying subject or idea of an instructional unit.

Toolbox: Part of the Standards-Based Thematic Unit Template, the Toolbox includes the Language Functions and Related Structures and Patterns, Vocabulary, and Resources needed to achieve the instructional goals of the unit.

Twenty-First Century Skills: Identified by business and education leaders, 21st Century Skills are the skills that students need to succeed in work, school, and life (www.p21.org).

Bibliography

American Council on the Teaching of Foreign Languages (ACTFL). (2012a). *ACTFL proficiency guidelines–speaking, writing, listening and reading*, (3rd ed.). Alexandria, VA: Author. Retrieved from http://actflproficiencyguidelines2012.org/

American Council on the Teaching of Foreign Languages (ACTFL). (2012b). *ACTFL performance descriptors for language learners.* Alexandria, VA: Author. Retrieved from http://www.acfl.org/publications/guidelines-and-manuals/actfl-performance-descriptors-language-learners

American Council on the Teaching of Foreign Languages (ACTFL). (2012c). *Alignment of the national standards for learning languages with the common core state standards.* Alexandria, VA: Author. Retrieved from http://www.actfl.org/sites/default/files/pdfs/Aligning_CCSS_Language_ Standards_v6.pdf

American Council on the Teaching of Foreign Languages (ACTFL). (2012, July 30). *Use of the target language in the classroom* [Press release]. Retrieved October 03, 2013, from http://www.actfl.org/news/position-statements/use-the-target-language-the-classroom

Ames, C. A. (1990). Motivation: What teachers need to know. *Teachers College Record, 91*(3), 409–421. Retrieved June 30, 2013, from http://web.uncg.edu/soe/bf_course669/docs_session_6/motivtion-whatteachersneedtoknow.pdf

Anderson, L. W., Krathwohl, D. R., & Bloom, B. S. (2001). *A taxonomy for learning, teaching, and assessing: A revision of Bloom's taxonomy of educational objectives.* New York: Longman.

Barcroft, J. (2004). Second language vocabulary acquisition: A lexical input processing approach. *Foreign Language Annals, 37*(2), 200–208.

Bergmann, J., Overmyer, J., & Wilie, B. (2012, April 14). The flipped class: Myths vs. reality. *The Daily Riff.* Retrieved June 24, 2013, from http://www.thedailyriff.com/articles/the-flipped-class-conversation-689.php

Bisson, C., & Luckner, J. (1996). Fun in learning: The pedagogical role of fun in adventure learning. *Journal of Experimental Education, 9*(2).

Bloom, B. S. (1956). *Taxonomy of educational objectives: The classification of educational goals.* New York: Longman.

Bloom's Digital Taxonomy. (n.d.). *Educational-origami.* Retrieved from http://edorigami.wikispaces.com/

Brandl, K. (2008). *Communicative language teaching in action: Putting principles to work.* Upper Saddle River, NJ: Pearson Prentice Hall.

Brookhart, S. M. (2012). Preventing feedback fizzle. *Educational Leadership, 70*(1), 25–29.

Brookhart, S. M. (2013). Assessing creativity. *Educational Leadership, 70*(5), 28–34.

Brookhart, S. M. (2013). *How to create and use rubrics for formative assessment and grading.* Alexandria, VA: ASCD.

Byram, M. (1997). *Teaching and assessing intercultural communicative competence.* Clevedon: Multilingual Matters.

Caine, R. N., & Caine, G. (1990). Understanding a brain-based approach to teaching and learning. *Educational Leadership, 48*(2), 66–70.

Carr, A. (2010, May 18). *The most important leadership quality for CEOs? Creativity.* Retrieved from http://www.fastcompany.com/1648943/most-important-leadership-quality-ceos-creativity.

Center for Excellence in Learning and Teaching. (n.d.). *CELT.* Retrieved from http://www.celt.iastate.edu/

Center for Media Literacy. (2011). *Media literacy: A definition and more.* Retrieved September 22, 2013, from http://www.medialit.org/media-literacy-definition-and-more

Collins, J. (2003, December 30). *Best new year's resolution? A 'stop doing' list.* Retrieved November 10, 2013, from http://www.jimcollins.com/article_topics/articles/best-new-years.html

Council of Europe. (2008). *White paper on intercultural dialogue: "Living together as equals in dignity."* Strasbourg, France: Council of Europe.

Crockett, L., Jukes, I., & Churches, A. (2011). *Literacy is not enough: 21st-century fluencies for the digital age.* Kelowna, B.C., Canada: 21st Century Fluency Project.

Crouse, D. (2012). Going for 90% plus: How to stay in the target language. *The Language Educator, 7*(5), 22–27.

Curtain, H. A., & Dahlberg, C. A. (2010). *Languages and children, making the match: New languages for young learners* (4th ed.). Boston: Pearson.

Cushman, K. (1994). Less is more: The secret of being essential. *Coalition of Essential Schools.* Retrieved July 07, 2013, from http://www.essentialschools.org/resources/34

Danesi, M. (2003). *Second language teaching: A view from the right side of the brain.* Dordrecht, The Netherlands: Kluwer Academic Publishers.

Danielson, L. M. (2009). Fostering reflection. *Education Leadership, 66*(5). Retrieved June 25, 2013, from http://www.ascd.org/publications/educational-leadership/feb09/vol66/num05/Fostering-Reflection.aspx

DeVoss, D. N., Eidman-Aadahl, E., & Hicks, T. (2010). *Because digital writing matters: Improving student writing in online and multimedia environments.* San Francisco: Jossey-Bass.

Dörnyei, Z. (2001). *Teaching and researching motivation.* Harlow, England: Longman.

Dörnyei, Z. (2005). *The psychology of the language learner: Individual differences in second language acquisition.* Mahwah, NJ: L. Erlbaum.

Dörnyei, Z., & Csizér, K. (1998). Ten commandments for motivating language learners: Results of an empirical study. *Language Teaching Research, 2*(3), 203–229.

Dougherty, E. (2012). *Assignments matter: Making the connections that help students meet standards.* Alexandria, VA: ASCD.

Duncan, G., & Met, M. (2010). *STARTALK: From paper to practice* (Publication). Retrieved June 10, 2013, from https://startalk.umd.edu/lesson-planning

Egan, K. (1986). *Individual development and the curriculum.* London: Hutchinson.

Fallows, D. (2010). *Dreaming in Chinese: Mandarin lessons in life, love, and language.* New York: Walker & Company.

Foreign Language Teaching Methods: The Language Learner. (n.d.). *Motivation predicts success.* Retrieved from http://coerll.utexas.edu/methods/modules/learners/02/

Fortune, T. (2012). Learning content through the target language. *Maintaining target language in the classroom: Comprehensible input and output* (Webinar Series). Alexandria, VA: ACTFL.

Gardner, H. (1983). *Frames of mind: The theory of multiple intelligences.* New York: Basic Books.

Gardner, H. (1999). *Intelligence reframed: Multiple intelligences for the 21st century.* New York: Basic Books.

Gardner, R. C. (1985). *Social psychology and second language learning: The role of attitudes and motivation.* London: E. Arnold.

Gardner, R. C., & Lambert, W. E. (1972). *Attitudes and motivation in second-language learning.* Rowley, MA: Newbury House.

Gewertz, C. (2013, April 8). Busting up misconceptions about formative 'assessment.' *Education Week.* Retrieved August 03, 2013, from http://blogs.edweek.org/edweek/curriculum/2013/04/httpwwwwestedorgonline_pubsres.html

Glaser, E. M. (1972). *An experiment in the development of critical thinking,.* New York: AMS Press.

Graham, C. R. (1985). Beyond integrative motivation: The development and influence of assimilative motivation. In *On TESOL '84: A brave new world for TESOL.* Washington, D.C.: TESOL.

Hale, S. L., & Cunningham, M. K. (2011). *Evidence based practice using a thematic based unit for language development.* Lecture. Retrieved July 26, 2013, from www.txsha.org

Hamilton, H. E., Crane, C., & Bartoshesky, A. (2005). *Doing foreign language: Bringing Concordia Language Villages into language classrooms.* Upper Saddle River, NJ: Pearson/Merrill/Prentice Hall.

Hattie, J. (2012). Know thy impact. *Educational Leadership, 70*(1), 18–23.

Himmele, P., & Himmele, W. (2011). *Total participation techniques: Making every student an active learner.* Alexandria, VA: ASCD.

Horwitz, E. K. (2008). *Becoming a language teacher: A practical guide to second language learning and teaching.* Boston: Pearson/Allyn and Bacon.

Hudelson, S. (1994). Literacy development of second language children. In F. Genesee (Ed.), *Educating second language children: The whole child, the whole curriculum, the whole community* (pp. 129–152). Cambridge: University Press.

Hunter, R. C., & Hunter, M. C. (2004). *Madeline Hunter's mastery teaching: Increasing instructional effectiveness in elementary and secondary schools.* Thousand Oaks, CA: Corwin Press.

Jacobson, W., Sleicher, D., & Burke, M. (1999). Portfolio assessment of intercultural competence. *International Journal of Intercultural Relations, 23*(3), 467–492.

Johnson, D. W., & Johnson, R. T. (1999). Making cooperative learning work. *Theory into Practice, 38*(2), 67–73.

Kramsch, C. J. (1993). *Context and culture in language teaching.* Oxford: Oxford University Press.

Krashen, S. D. (1982). *Principles and practice in second language acquisition.* Oxford: Pergamon.

LeLoup, J. W., Ponterio, R., & Warford, M. K. (2013). Overcoming resistance to 90% target language use: Rationale, challenges, and suggestions. *NECTFL Review, 72,* 45–60.

Lent, R.C. (2012). *Overcoming textbook fatigue: 21st century tools to revitalize teaching and learning.* Alexandria, VA: ASCD.

LinguaFolio–National Council of State Supervisors for Languages. (n.d.). *LinguaFolio–National Council of State Supervisors for Languages.* Retrieved from http://www.ncssfl.org/links/index.php?linguafolio

LinguaFolio online. Retrieved October 31, 2013 from https://linguafolio.uoregon.edu/

Little D. & Perclová, R. (2001). *The European language portfolio: A guide for teachers and teacher trainers.* Strasbourg, France: Council of Europe, Language Policy Division.

Little, D. & Simpson, B. (2003). *European language portfolio: The intercultural component and learning how to learn.* Strasbourg, France: Council of Europe.

Macintyre, P. D. (2007). Willingness to communicate in the second language: Understanding the decision to speak as a volitional process. *The Modern Language Journal, 91*(4), 564–576.

Marzano, R. J. (2006). *Classroom assessment & grading that work.* Alexandria, VA: ASCD.

Marzano, R. J. (2007). *The art and science of teaching: A comprehensive framework for effective instruction.* Alexandria, VA: ASCD.

McTighe, J., & Wiggins, G. P. (2013). *Essential questions: Opening doors to student understanding.* Alexandria: ASCD.

Media habits of teens and twenty-somethings 2012. (2012, July). Retrieved from http://www.google.com/think/research-studies/media-habits-of-teens-and-twenty-somethings-2012.html

Mickan, P. (2013). *Language curriculum design and socialisation.* Bristol: Multilingual Matters.

Minerva Programme. (n.d.). Project of study of the electronic European Language Portfolio. Retrieved from http://eelp.gap.it/default.asp.

Moeller, A. J., & Ketsman, O. (2010). Can we learn a language without rules? *In 2020 Vision for 2010: Developing Global Competence* (pp. 91–108). Richmond, VA: Robert Terry.

Moss, C. M., & Brookhart, S. M. (2012). *Learning targets: Helping students aim for understanding in today's lesson.* Alexandria, VA: ASCD.

National Capital Language Resource Center (NCLRC). 2003. Method: Learner-centered instruction. In *The essentials of language teaching: Teaching goals and methods.* Retrieved from http://www.nclrc.org/essentials/goalsmethods/method.htm

National Governors Association Center for Best Practices, Council of Chief State School Officers (CCSSO). (2010). *Common core state standards for English language arts and literacy in history/social studies, science, and technical subjects.* Washington, DC: Author.

National Standards in Foreign Language Education Project (NSFLEP). (1996). *Standards for foreign language learning: Preparing for the 21st century.* Yonkers, NY: Author.

National Standards in Foreign Language Education Project (NSFLEP). (1999). *Standards for foreign language learning in the 21st century* (2nd ed.). Lawrence, KS: Allen Press.

National Standards in Foreign Language Education Project (NSFLEP). (2006). *Standards for foreign language learning in the 21st century* (3rd ed.). Lawrence, KS: Allen Press.

NCTE position statements on literacy. (2013, February). *NCTE Comprehensive News.* Retrieved from http://www.ncte.org/positions/literacy

Oxford, R. L. (1990). *Language learning strategies: What every teacher should know.* New York: Newbury House Publisher.

The Partnership for 21st Century Skills. (n.d.). *Framework for 21st century learning.* Retrieved from http://www.p21.org/overview/skills-framework

Pink, D. H. (2009). *Drive: The surprising truth about what motivates us.* New York, NY: Riverhead Books.

Prensky, M. (2002). The motivation of gameplay: The real twenty-first century learning revolution. *On the Horizon, 10*(1), 5–11.

Prensky, M. (2012, May/June). *Teaching the right stuff.* Retrieved October 31, 2013 from http://marcprensky.com/writing/Prensky-TheRightStuff-EdTech-May-Jun2012.pdf

Robinson, K. (2011). *Out of our minds: Learning to be creative.* Oxford: Capstone.

Schmoker, M. J. (2011). *Focus: Elevating the essentials to radically improve student learning.* Alexandria, VA: ASCD.

Schulz, R. (2007). The challenge of assessing cultural understanding in the context of foreign language instruction. *Foreign Language Annals, 40*(1), 9–20.

Selivan, L. (2010, September). Revising lexis: Quality or quantity? *Teaching English | British Council | BBC*. Retrieved July 28, 2013, from http://www.teachingenglish.org.uk/

Shrum, J. L., & Glisan, E. W. (2010). *Teacher's handbook: Contextualized language instruction* (4th ed.). Boston, MA: Heinle.

Sousa, D. A. (2006). *How the brain learns*. Thousand Oaks, CA: Corwin Press.

Tedick, D. J. (2002). *The Minnesota articulation project's proficiency-oriented language instruction and assessment: A curriculum handbook for teachers*. Minneapolis, MN: Center for Advanced Research on Language Acquisition, University of Minnesota.

Tomlinson, C. A. (1999). *The differentiated classroom: Responding to the needs of all learners*. Alexandria, VA: ASCD.

Tprstories.com. (n.d.). Retrieved from http://www.tprsstories.com/

Trilling, B., & Fadel, C. (2009). *21st century skills: Learning for life in our times*. San Francisco: Jossey-Bass.

Tuttle, H. G., & Tuttle, A. R. (2012). *Improving foreign language speaking through formative assessment*. Larchmont, NY: Eye on education.

Vatterott, C. (2009). *Rethinking homework: Best practices that support diverse needs*. Alexandria, VA: ASCD.

Welcome to LEARN NC! (n.d.). *LEARN NC*. Retrieved from http://www.learnnc.org/lp/editions/linguafolio/6122

Wiggins, G. (2012). 7 keys to effective feedback. *Educational Leadership, 70*(1), 11–16.

Wiggins, G. P., & McTighe, J. (1998). *Understanding by design*. Alexandria, VA: ASCD.

Wiggins, G. P., & McTighe, J. (2005). *Understanding by design* (2nd ed.). Alexandria, VA: ASCD.

Willis, J. (2005). Attention to have and to hold. *Journal of the National Council of Teachers of English, 8–9*. Retrieved May 29, 2013, from http://www.radteach.com/page1/page8/page9/page9.html

Willis, J. (2006). *Research-based strategies to ignite student learning: Insights from a neurologist and classroom teacher*. Alexandria, VA: ASCD.

World languages 21st century skills map. (n.d.). Retrieved from http://www.p21.org/storage/documents/Skills%20Map/p21_worldlanguagesmap.pdf

Ziegler, N. A., & Moeller, A. J. (2012). Increasing self-regulated learning through the LinguaFolio. *Foreign Language Annals, 45*(3), 330–348.

Zilmer, C. (2013). 90%+ target language, authentic texts, no isolated grammar? How? *The Language Educator, 8*(3), 26–29.